Complete Audio-Typing: Teacher's Book
A Programmed Course

Marion Prescott, B.A.(Hons), M.Sc.(Econ), M.B.I.M.
Head of Department of Office Studies
South East London College

Pitman

PITMAN PUBLISHING LIMITED
128 Long Acre,
London WC2E 9AN

A Longman Group Company

British Library Cataloguing in Publication Data

Prescott, Marion
    Pitman complete audio typing. — 2nd ed.
    Teacher's book
    1. Typewriting — Problems, exercises, etc.
    I.   Title
    652.3'07   Z49.2

ISBN 0 273 02544 9

Acknowledgements

I should like to thank my colleagues in the Inner
London service for their help, encouragement and co-
operation in validating the material.

I should also like to thank the Royal Society of Arts
for their kind permission to reproduce examination
papers in Audio Typewriting.

Produced by Longman Singapore Publishers (Pte) Ltd.
Printed in Singapore

Introduction to Teacher's Book

A teacher using this course will need both the Teacher's Book, and, for ease of checking, the Student's Book. Each student MUST have a copy of the Student's Book.

The Teacher's Book contains a complete programmed course of dictation material progressing from simple sentences to advanced office dictation. All the instructions to students are given and the material is prepared, making use of the Royal Society of Arts dictating conventions, where appropriate. All the teacher needs to do is to make the master cassettes and arrange for the dubbing of the required number of copies. Pre-recorded cassettes may be purchased ready for use with certain manufacturers' models.

The Student's Book consists of all the dictated exercise material (except production tasks, which the teacher checks and which are set out in this Book). The material is displayed so that the student checks her own work as she proceeds. Thus she has complete control of her own machine and works at her own pace. The student corrects her own work and is instructed to audio-type it again (but not copy type) if she makes more than a specified number of uncorrected errors. The teacher may wish to re-check this work. However, the only essential correcting the teacher must do is of the student's production tasks which are given regularly (every third or fourth task) to test progress.

The major points of information are given in the Student's Book in Reference Sections 1 to 12 (covering, for example, letter display, use of the apostrophe, indicator slips, etc.). These reference sections introduce and explain the main areas of work. They can each be used as the basis of a class lesson. Most teachers would agree that there is a need for class lessons, not only because some of the reference sections are fairly difficult, but also to stimulate interest and class spirit, particularly as the student works largely on her own. When using a reference section as the basis of a class lesson, it must be borne in mind, of course, that the students are not all at the same point in the course. This does not cause difficulty since each student is instructed (by the cassette) to study the appropriate reference section before proceeding to the tasks. Thus the student can either revise the section (if this comes after the class lesson) or can prepare in advance — the class lesson becoming the opportunity for revision, question and explanation. The student's work settles to a pattern:

(*a*) study (or revise) reference section
(*b*) read notes to task
(*c*) audio-type task
(*d*) correct task
(*e*) if necessary, repeat (*a*) to (*d*)
(*f*) audio-type Production task for teacher to mark

Thus, this course provides the teacher with a complete set of material for training of audio-typists.

Equipment necessary for this course

The whole aim of this approach is to allow the student to progress at her own pace and in complete control of her own machine. A master control unit or four-channel system is therefore not necessary. However, unless it is wished to purchase sufficient pre-recorded cassettes, dubbing facilities are needed.

Preparation of media

There is up to 15 minutes dictation material in each Unit. It is counted at 70 wpm up to RSA I papers, and at 80 wpm thereafter. Half-minutes are shown.

When dictating it is very important that the natural inflexions of the voice are retained. Shorthand-style dictation is a positive handicap to an audio-typist who, rather than simply trying to "get it down", is listening and trying to UNDERSTAND what is heard. For example, short sentences should be dictated as whole units, and long sentences broken down into long phrases. The timings are there only as a guide to planning the media and should not be carefully timed with a stopwatch.

It is recommended that the actual cassette, as well as any container, is clearly numbered in sequence. For example, the first side of the first cassette may be labelled: 1; the second side: 2; the first side of the second cassette: 3; the second side of the second cassette: 4; and so on. Thus, if a cassette is left out of its container, it is known exactly what is on it.

When dictating, you should note, at the beginning of each task, the point on the scale or index at which the machine starts. You can complete the dotted lines in the Teacher's Book given for this purpose.

Number of cassettes required

For the first batch of tasks the maximum number of cassettes will be required. That is, if 20 students are to be trained on 20 machines, 20 cassettes of the first set of tasks will be needed. Thereafter you will probably need the full number of copies of the second cassette, 15 of the third cassette, but 10 will probably be sufficient for subsequent sets, because the students work at their own pace, and the demand "spreads out" as the lessons progress. If resources are very limited half the class can start off ahead of the other half (who can revise typing display), so that the spread is even greater. The complete course runs for 8 × 15-minute cassettes, using both sides.

Use of the Teacher's and Student's book

Since model tasks are given in the Student's Book, the teacher will need to impress on the students how important it is to use the Student's Book intelligently – and not to look at the answers when producing their work. The teacher will need to watch the class carefully to check that students do not copy-type their finished versions. However, an independent check on each student's progress is provided by the production tasks, which occur every third or fourth task, model tasks to which are given only in the Teacher's Book. Since the students work most of the time as individuals, it is important that their progress is carefully monitored. It is suggested that the Progress Record be completed by the students at the end of each lesson, so that they can clearly see at which point they should start when they next come to use the course. The teacher may also complete the Production Task Record on marking each production task. Both of these forms are given in the Student's Book, but if class sets of books have to be used rather than personal copies, the teacher may wish to duplicate them – preferably on thin, coloured card.

The fully-blocked, open-punctuated method of display has been adopted for the majority of tasks in the Student's Book. Specific instructions on the style of display for each letter or memo are not given and students should use the style to which they are accustomed. Reference sections on display, giving alternatives, are given in the Student's Book. Instructions regarding margins to be used are not normally given. It is assumed that students know which margins to use, though this may need revision, particularly before students go on to type letters.

The most up-to-date methods of punctuation and numbering are given in the Student's Book. All numbers are typed as figures (unless otherwise instructed) except the number one, or where a number begins a sentence. Ordinal numbers are typed as words, with only a few exceptions, where an instruction is normally given. It is not necessary for students to use this system, though they should understand it from the point of view of checking their work. In the Teacher's Book, traditional punctuation is maintained, and numbers are spelled out as words, for ease of dictation.

Commas are used extensively in the Teacher's Book, to aid the dictation, but only the more important commas are shown in the Student's Book: it is suggested that omission of inessential commas should not be penalized, but incorrect insertion of commas (where they are not needed) should be penalized.

Planning the course

The teacher needs to plan the course so that the slowest students will complete what are considered to be the most important parts of the book. This will depend on the educational/training aims for those students. More advanced students, who complete the course quickly, can work on additional examination papers (available from the various examination bodies) or realistic office dictation, prepared by a variety of people, making use of regional accents, etc.

Educational standards of students

This book is for teaching audio-typing and transcription skills. It is essential, therefore, that the students are reasonably literate. A considerable number of points of difficulty in the use of English are revised and reinforced in the tasks, and the "less-able" students can gain a lot from working the early tasks. However, in the author's opinion, the minimum standard of English required for completion of the course is equivalent to CSE Grade 3. For intensive courses, GCE O level is the preferred standard.

Students will also need to have mastered the keyboard and be able to type accurately to approximately 25 words a minute. Typing theory is revised in the instructions to each task but it is assumed that the students have covered the basic display appropriate to each section of the work.

Approaches to audio-training

The "intensive" approach

This book can be used intensively to train part-time students who are already competent typists, have a reasonable standard of English, and have completed their office training as typists. Able students can work an intensive version of the book by completing only one practice passage (instead of two or three) before each production task.

The "integrated" approach

Most teachers of full-time students will use this approach, as it reinforces the teaching of typewriting, English, and shorthand transcription. By "integrated" I mean that audio-typewriting is part of the student's typewriting study, the student spending a few hours a week on audio-typewriting after completing the keyboard stage, and as her knowledge of typewriting display proceeds.

The integrated approach is of considerable value in the training of secretaries. The transcription training (if carried out as in this book) is easier for an audio-typist than for a shorthand-typist, as she does not have to concentrate on making sense of her shorthand. As long as the recordings have been dubbed clearly, the audio-typing student should understand what she is typing. Thus she can give her attention exclusively to correct display, grammar and spelling. Having mastered the pitfalls of audio-transcription, she will be much more competent to proceed to shorthand transcription and can give her full attention to the meaning of her shorthand.

Teacher's notes to the first lesson

It is very difficult to manage with lessons of less than one hour. Setting up and packing away equipment each takes about 10 minutes. Ideally a two-hour period is best, but the students should have a short break from listening about half-way through the lesson.

Firstly, the students must see an audio machine ready for operation with footpedal and headset plugged in and the index set at nought on the scale. If possible, the teacher should demonstrate audio-typing, showing how the typing is continuous, but listening only intermittent.

As with the first lesson in typing, it is a very good idea to have the machines all completely ready for use. The assembly of the machine and the operation of the controls is rather a lot for the student to learn at one time. Where at all possible, assembly should be done in advance.

If the machines are connected ready for use, the teacher has only to demonstrate the operation of the footpedal to play and to backtrack for repetition purposes; also to demonstrate the index on the machine. The students will be keen to start and they can go straight on to the listening exercise.

If you need to introduce a class to the assembly and use of the machine in the first lesson, it is very important to do this very slowly and calmly. Make the whole class perform one operation at a time, and check that everyone has completed this before moving to the next stage. Emphasize that care must be taken with equipment which is plugged into the electricity mains.

Introduce the important rule of always starting with the cassette at the beginning and the index set at nought. It is not necessary to introduce methods of indexing at this stage, except by way of general explanation.

At a suitable point in the lesson it is a good idea to get the students to pack away all the equipment, noting carefully what they are doing. When this is complete you can spend a few minutes discussing job opportunities for audio-typists, etc., and then ask the students to re-assemble their machines. This can be done as a class operation or individually, with the teacher giving appropriate help and instructions. Students could be asked to complete a flow chart for machine assembly.

The amount of audio work completed in the first lesson will be very little, but will, of course, depend on the type of student and the amount of time allocated. The control of the machines, the listening exercise and a short discussion will, with average students, take at least an hour.

Checking the equipment

Invariably, at least one student will, at some time, have a cassette that "does not work". Never take her word for it! First check that the machine is on, the volume up, and the headset and footpedal connected correctly. If this fails, make an independent check of the equipment.

It is recommended that the teacher has her own equipment, which she knows is in perfect working order, set up in the classroom. She can then test the cassette on this. If the cassette is satisfactory, she can then test the headset, then the footpedal, and finally the machine itself, against her own equipment — thus isolating the faulty item. It is suggested that the teacher keeps a "dumping box" into which can be put any cassette or item of equipment which does not appear to function, and thus keep them separate from the rest of the equipment.

The following materials are needed for each lesson:

1 independently-operated audio machine, headset and footpedal per student and, of course, one typewriter per student

1 dictionary per student

Supply of A4 and A5 typing paper: carbon paper when appropriate

Supply of headed A4 and A5 paper, when appropriate — if available

1 cassette per student (see page 1 — number of cassettes required)

1 copy of Student's Book per student

1 copy of Teacher's Book for reference purposes

Audio-Typing: Programmed

Instructions to dictator: Dictate everything (including punctuation which is typed out in full) with the exception of instructions to you — which are in CLOSED CAPITALS within rounded brackets. Dictate at an average speed of 70 wpm but preserve the natural inflexions of the voice.

DICTATION STARTS NOW

The first task of this course is a listening exercise. You do not need to type yet. Adjust your volume control, if necessary. I am going to tell you some facts about audio-typing. There will be ten sentences altogether and after each sentence I shall ask you a question. Say the answer to yourself. Listen carefully. Are you ready?

(EMPHASIZE UNDERSCORED WORDS)

1. There are many good, well-paid jobs open to audio-typists nowadays and the most competent girls can become audio-secretaries.
Question: What can good audio-typists become?
(PAUSE – 5 SECONDS APPROX.)
The answer is: audio-secretaries.

2. In most offices shorthand-typists are expected to be able to audio-type in addition to their other skills.
Question: What are most shorthand-typists expected to do in addition to shorthand?
(PAUSE – 5 SECONDS APPROX.)
The answer is: audio-type.

3. An audio-typist types what she hears, and must listen carefully so that she understands what she types.
Question: Why must you listen carefully?
(PAUSE – 5 SECONDS APPROX.)
The answer is: to understand what you type.

4. If an audio-typist does not understand what she hears she must listen again by backtracking her machine.
Question: What must you do if you do not understand?
(PAUSE – 5 SECONDS APPROX.)
The answer is: listen again by backtracking.

5. An audio-typist listens to a whole sentence or a very long phrase before beginning to type.
Question: How much should you listen to before typing?
(PAUSE – 5 SECONDS APPROX.)
The answer is: a whole sentence or very long phrase.

6. A skilled audio-typist will be listening to the beginning of the second sentence while typing the end of the first one.
Question: What is the skilled audio-typist listening to when typing the end of the first sentence?
(PAUSE – 5 SECONDS APPROX.)
The answer is: the beginning of the second sentence.

7. Continuous typing is the aim of a skilled audio-typist, who listens and types at the same time.
Question: What is listening and typing at the same time called?
(PAUSE – 5 SECONDS APPROX.)
The answer is: continuous typing.

8. An audio-typist always has a dictionary on her desk to check any difficult spellings.
Question: What should you always have on your desk?
(PAUSE – 5 SECONDS APPROX.)
The answer is: a dictionary.

9. An audio-typist always looks at the work being typed so that she checks it as she produces it.
Question: What do you look at when audio-typing?
(PAUSE – 5 SECONDS APPROX.)
The answer is: the work being typed.

10. An audio-typist corrects any errors when she makes them, and always checks her work again before taking it out of her typewriter.
Question: When do you correct your errors?
(PAUSE – 5 SECONDS APPROX.)
The answer is: when you make them.

(PAUSE)

Unit One

You should now be used to the sound of my voice and ready to start typing, but first look at the notes to Task one one in your book. I shall dictate 5 sentences. Do not begin to type each sentence until you have heard the whole of it. Wait until you hear the words "full stop" before starting to type each sentence. Don't forget to start each one with a capital letter, and to correct your mistakes as you go along. Are you ready?

(POINT ON INDEX IS . . .)

We thank you for your order for our products. **(full stop, new line)**
We regret that we have completely sold out. **(full stop, new line)**
There was a very heavy demand for these goods. **(full stop, new line)**
Our workers were on overtime for several months. / **(full stop, ½ new line)**
We hope to despatch your order next week. **(full stop)**

(PAUSE)

Check your work from Model Task one one in your book. Check every single word. Put a circle around each uncorrected error you made. If you have made more than two, put a clean piece of paper in your machine, close your book, put your first attempt out of sight, and start again. You must audio-type it again and not simply copy-type. I began dictating Task one at . . . on your index, so if you need to audio-type it again go back to that point.

I am now going to dictate another five sentences for you to type. This is Task one two. Start each sentence on a new line. Remember not to start typing each sentence until you hear the words "full stop". Ready?

(POINT ON INDEX IS . . .)

We have just received your letter with enclosures. **(full stop)**
We are very pleased with the new designs. **(full stop)**
We think these will appeal to our younger customers. **(full stop)**
We shall forward the designs to our branches. **(full stop)**
We hope / to place our order in due course. **(full stop)**   ½

(PAUSE)

Check your work from Model Task one two in your book. Check every single word. As before, if you have made more than two uncorrected errors, you should audio-type the task again. I began dictating Task one two at . . . .

I shall now dictate another five sentences. This is a production task and your paper should be headed with your name and the words "Production Task A". You should time yourself to see how many minutes you take. You are to type it once only

and give it directly to your teacher for marking. Are you ready for Production Task A?

(POINT ON INDEX IS . . .)

I hope you are enjoying your first lesson. **(full stop)**
There will be many good jobs open to you. **(full stop)**
You will find advertisements in all the newspapers. **(full stop)**
You can earn a very good salary. **(full stop)**
I think you / will find the work interesting. **(full stop)**   ½

(PAUSE)

Make sure you have headed your paper before handing it to your teacher to mark. After marking it, your teacher will note the mark on your Record Sheet.

I shall now dictate further short sentence practice. This is Task one three. Are you ready?

(POINT ON INDEX IS . . .)

We would like you to study the enclosed literature. **(full stop)**
Full details of our latest range are given. **(full stop)**
These products are offered at very good discounts. **(full stop)**
There is a good market for these products locally. **(full stop)**
Please / let us know if you are interested. **(full stop)**   ½

(PAUSE)

Check your work from Model Task one three in your book, and if necessary audio-type it again. I began dictating Task one three at . . . .

I shall now dictate further short sentence practice. This is Task one four. Are you ready?

(POINT ON INDEX IS . . .)

Thank you for your recent letter with enclosed order. **(full stop)**
We are sorry to say we no longer manufacture these goods. **(full stop)**
We now make a product of slightly different design. **(full stop)**
We are enclosing some leaflets for your attention. **(full stop)**
We look forward to hearing further from you. / **(full stop)**   ½

(PAUSE)

Check your work from Model Task one four in your book, and if necessary audio-type it again. I began dictating Task one four at . . . .

End of Unit One

Unit Two

I am now going to dictate five longer sentences and I want you to do something slightly different. Instead of listening to the whole sentence before beginning to type, I should like you to start typing after you have heard the first long phrase, at which point I shall pause a second. But before you finish typing the first phrase, I want you to start your machine again and listen to the rest of the sentence whilst continuing to type. If you do this successfully, you will be typing each sentence continuously. These instructions are repeated in the notes to Task two one in your book. Ready?

(POINT ON INDEX IS . . .)

We have received your request concerning colour televisions **(PAUSE)** and are enclosing full details. **(full stop)**
You will notice that our cheapest model is good value **(PAUSE)** when compared with those of our competitors. **(full stop)**
At the other end of / the list is our luxury model **(PAUSE)** ½ which is superior to any other on the market. **(full stop)**
We think your customers will like our sets **(PAUSE)** as we have the best range on offer. **(full stop)**
We look forward to // hearing from you **(PAUSE)** and hope 1 that you will place a trial order. **(full stop)**

(PAUSE)

Check your work from Model Task two one in your book. Are you managing to type all the time right through each sentence? If you have made more than two uncorrected errors, or if you feel you need more practice at continuous typing, go back to . . . on your index and audio-type those sentences again.
There now follow five long sentences similar to those in the last task. Aim to type right through each sentence, but remember to listen to the first long phrase before beginning to type. Are you ready for Task two two?

(POINT ON INDEX IS . . .)

Thank you for your enquiry concerning holidays abroad **(PAUSE)** for which I am enclosing brochures. **(full stop)**
This year we have a variety of holidays **(PAUSE)** which we are sure will interest you. **(full stop)**
You may like a sunny holiday / on the coast **(PAUSE)** or perhaps ½ a quiet rest in pleasant surroundings. **(full stop)**
Our brochure lists only the very best hotels **(PAUSE)** at which you can be sure of good service. **(full stop)**
You should return the booking form immediately **(PAUSE)** to // make sure you are not disappointed. **(full stop)** 1

(PAUSE)

Check your work from Model Task two two in your book. I began dictating that task at . . . .
The next five sentences are similar to those you have typed in the previous task. This is Production Task B for your teacher to mark. Remember, you must type it once only. Make a note of how many minutes you take and aim at continuous typing. Have you headed the paper with your name and the task number? Ready?

(POINT ON INDEX IS . . .)

We apologise for the delay in replying to your letter **(PAUSE)** which we received only today. **(full stop)**
The goods you require are not in stock **(PAUSE)** and will not be delivered until next month. **(full stop)**
In the meantime we / could send you some similar styles ½ **(PAUSE)** which are certain to meet with your approval. **(full stop)**
If you would like us to forward these items **(PAUSE)** please telephone our local branch immediately. **(full stop)**
We are sorry we cannot meet // your exact requirements 1 **(PAUSE)** but hope our suggestion will help you. **(full stop)**

(PAUSE)

Make sure the number of minutes you took is on the bottom of your paper before giving it to your teacher to check.
I shall now dictate further long sentence practice. This is Task two three. Ready?

(POINT ON INDEX IS . . .)

Thank you for your recent letter **(PAUSE)** and for returning your copy of the inventory. **(full stop)**
We are pleased to hear that you enjoyed your holiday **(PAUSE)** and that the caravan was in a good location. **(full stop)**
We are refunding your deposit **(PAUSE)** with an additional amount to pay for the broken chair. **(full stop)**
We / agree that the chair needed replacing **(PAUSE)** and that ½ you are not responsible for the extra charge. **(full stop)**
We look forward to receiving a booking from you for next year **(PAUSE)** and will send you the new brochure // soon. **(full 1 stop)**

(PAUSE)

Check your work from Model Task two three in your book, and if necessary audio-type it again. I began dictating Task two three at . . . .
I shall now dictate further long sentence practice. This is Task two four. Ready?

(POINT ON INDEX IS . . .)

Thank you for your order for our kitchen equipment **(PAUSE)** which will be despatched during the next few days. **(full stop)**
We do not have any storage jars in stock at the moment **(PAUSE)** but we will send these / to you as soon as possible. ½ **(full stop)**
We can give you a refund for these goods immediately **(PAUSE)** if you prefer not to wait. **(full stop)**
We are enclosing our new catalogue and price list **(PAUSE)** from which you will // see that some new lines are available. 1 **(full stop)**

We are pleased to say that most of our goods **(PAUSE)** cost the same price as that charged last year. **(full stop)**

(PAUSE)

Check your work from Model Task two four in your book, and if necessary audio-type it again. I began dictating Task two four at . . . .

End of Unit Two

Unit Three

I am now going to dictate three short paragraphs. Remember to look at the notes to Task three one in your book. These paragraphs are to be typed continuously, which means that, although you listen only some of the time, you should aim at typing all the time. Before you finish typing each long phrase or short sentence, you should start your machine again and listen to the next section so that you type right through. I shall tell you when to start a new paragraph.

Are you ready for Task three one?

(POINT ON INDEX IS . . .)

I was very interested to hear of the book **(PAUSE)** which you are writing about your childhood. **(full stop)** I am sure that the public will be very interested **(PAUSE)** in the life of such a famous sportsman. **(paragraph)**

I / should like to have a meeting with you to discuss the book. **(full stop)** We could either meet at my office in town **(PAUSE)** or at your home in the country. **(full stop)** Please let me know which you prefer. // **(paragraph)**   ½

I very much look forward to meeting you. **(full stop)** I should be grateful if you would telephone me **(PAUSE)** to arrange a suitable time and date. **(full stop)** I look forward to hearing further from you. **(full stop)**   1

(PAUSE)

Check your work from Model Task three one in your book. Are you managing to type each paragraph continuously? If you are, you can go on to the next task, but if you feel you need further practice go back to . . . on your index.

I shall now dictate some more paragraphs for you to type continuously, but, before starting, you should look at the notes to Task three two and then study Reference Section One. Ready?

(POINT ON INDEX IS . . .)

I shall write to Mr. John Brown and thank him for his letter. **(full stop)** He wrote saying that he could not attend the interview next Tuesday. **(full stop)** He can come at the same time on Thursday. **(paragraph)**

I / / think we should hold the interview at our new offices in Oxford Street. **(full stop)** It will be easy for Mr. Brown to get there as he lives in Harrow. **(full stop)** He will be able to travel in // by car or on the underground. **(paragraph)**   ½   1

Mr. Brown will work at our Birmingham factory if he is appointed. **(full stop)** It is important to point this out to Mr. Brown at the interview. **(full stop)** He may not wish / to move so far if he has children of school age. **(paragraph)**   ½

(PAUSE)

Check your work from Model Task three two in your book. Did you use capital letters correctly? I began dictating that task at . . . .

I shall now dictate three more paragraphs for you to type continuously, but before starting you should look at the notes to Task three three in your book. Are you ready for Task three three?

(POINT ON INDEX IS . . .)

We have written to Mr. K. Smith to invite him to a meeting of our **(initial capitals)** Sales Representatives. **(full stop)** The meeting will be held in the **(initial capitals)** Board Room on Friday next. **(full stop)** Lunch will be served before the / meeting. **(paragraph)**   ½

Mr. Smith used to work for a large American firm at their London office. **(full stop)** The position he held was **(initial capitals)** International Sales Director of the **(initial capital)** Company. **(full stop)** He will therefore have much to say of value // to our Sales Representatives. **(paragraph)**   1

We hope Mr. Smith can advise us on the introduction of our new product to the British market. **(full stop)** We do not think he is interested in a permanent job in this / country. **(full stop)** ½ We might consider appointing him as a **(initial capital)** Consultant to our **(initial capital)** Company.

(PAUSE)

Check your work from Model Task three three in your book. Did you remember to type "Sales Representatives" with capitals the **second** time this was dictated? I began dictating that task at . . . .

The next task is a production task for your teacher to mark. Make a note of the number of minutes you take, and aim at continuous typing. Are your name and "Production Task C" at the top of your paper?

(POINT ON INDEX IS . . .)

At the recent **(initial capitals)** Annual General Meeting of British Products Limited the **(initial capital)** Chairman presented the **(initial capitals)** Report and Accounts for the year. **(paragraph)**

The Chairman said that the figures for the year were very good indeed. **(full stop)** He pointed / out that the **(initial capital)** ½ Company had done considerably better than other firms manufacturing similar products. **(full stop)** This was a very satisfactory result after the poor figures for last year. **(paragraph)**

The Chairman continued by saying that he thought // there was **1** considerable potential for further growth of the Company. **(full stop)** He thanked the **(initial capital)** Directors and all the employees of the Company for their hard work. **(full stop)** He concluded by saying that progress was only possible when / ½ there was loyalty and enthusiasm among staff at all levels.

(PAUSE)

Remember that production tasks are to be typed once only, so give your first attempt to your teacher to mark, noting on the bottom how many minutes you took. Always re-check your work for typing mistakes before handing it in.

I shall now dictate further short paragraph practice. This is Task three four. Ready?

(POINT ON INDEX IS ...)

We have received a brochure from the local travel agency and are interested in flights to the United States. **(full stop)** We are not yet sure whether it would be best to fly to New York or Washington. / **(paragraph)** ½

It is not clear from the literature which airports are used by these flights and we wonder whether they are from Gatwick or Heathrow. **(full stop)** It would be easier for us to get to Gatwick Airport // as we live in Brighton. **(paragraph)** 1

When we are in America we would like to hire a car. **(full stop)** We understand that it is easy to do this with companies such as Avis and Hertz. **(full stop)** Can you / confirm that the booking ½ and payment can be made here and the car collected from the airport in the States?

(PAUSE)

Check your work from Model Task three four in your book, and if necessary audio-type it again. I began dictating Task three four at . . . . .

End of Unit Three

Unit Four

I am now going to dictate three short paragraphs. Remember to look at the notes to Task four one in your book. These paragraphs contain a number of plural words and you should study Reference Section Two before starting. Are you now ready for Task four one?

(POINT ON INDEX IS . . .)

We have heard from our suppliers in Hong Kong that several cargoes of radios should reach us in January. **(full stop)** These are packed in cardboard boxes with a dozen in each of the crates. **(paragraph)**

In addition / to the radios there will be a consignment of quartz ½ watches. **(full stop)** These come in several styles for both men and women. **(full stop)** There is also a range for children which feature pictures of their latest screen // heroes on the 1 watch faces. **(paragraph)**

We are only one of several companies importing these goods. **(full stop)** We think that the prices are excellent and that they will sell throughout the cities and counties of the UK / without ½ difficulty. **(full stop)** There will be no exclusive agencies for these products.

(PAUSE)

Check your work from Model Task four one in your book. Pay special attention to the plural words. If you have made more than two uncorrected errors, you should audio-type that task again. I began dictating Task four one at . . . on the index.

I shall now dictate three more paragraphs. As well as containing some plural words, these paragraphs also contain the instruction "initial capital". See the notes to Task four two before commencing. Are you ready?

(POINT ON INDEX IS . . .)

We are interested in purchasing some new word processors which your **(initial capital)** Company is marketing. **(full stop)** We would like further information on the complete range of models. **(paragraph)**

Can you ask one of your **(initial capitals)** Sales Representatives to call. / **(full stop)** It would be best if he telephoned my **(initial** ½ **capital)** Secretary first to make a firm appointment. **(paragraph)**

We are looking for models which will be easy to operate and which our secretaries can learn to use without // difficulty. **(full** 1 **stop)** We notice that you supply machines made by firms such as Wang and IBM. **(full stop)** We now believe we should be replacing all our electric typewriters with word processors or electronic machines. / ½

(PAUSE)

Check your work from Model Task four two in your book. If you have made more than two uncorrected errors you should audio-type it again. I began dictating Task four two at . . . .

I am now going to dictate Production Task D. Please read the notes to this task before commencing. Are you ready?

(POINT ON INDEX IS . . .)

There have been a number of bankruptcies in our town in the last few years and many people have become unemployed. **(full stop)** So far our own company has survived several major crises. **(paragraph)**

Many companies have / closed down and this affects the trade ½ for local shops and services. **(full stop)** Firms may get into financial difficulties. **(full stop)** Fortunately our own business is not affected by a general slump in trade. **(paragraph)**

We hope that business // prospects generally will improve 1 soon. **(full stop)** There will be a need for much investment in declining cities and other localities. **(full stop)** There will need to be an improvement in the facilities we offer to other businesses. / ½

(PAUSE)

Make a note of the time you took and hand your work directly to your teacher for marking.

I shall now dictate further paragraph practice. This is Task four three. Are you ready?

(POINT ON INDEX IS . . .)

The number of women senior directors in most businesses is usually very small. **(full stop)** Most women directors are traditionally found in the area of personnel management. **(full stop)** Probably the best way for women to get into senior / ½ management is through obtaining university degrees or professional qualifications. **(paragraph)**

Many graduates wanting to get into business will find that it is worthwhile to obtain secretarial qualifications. **(full stop)** This is particularly true if careers in the publishing // industry or the 1 media are of interest. **(paragraph)**

Secretarial skills are undoubtedly useful in themselves. **(full stop)** The ability to type accurately and quickly is a real asset when using computers. **(full stop)** A good knowledge of office systems and equipment / is also very useful. **(full stop)** Short- ½ hand can be of considerable benefit in meetings and when drafting reports. **(full stop)** Many women managers who have progressed from secretarial positions value their secretarial skills highly.

(PAUSE)

Check your work from Model Task four three in your book. If you have made more than two uncorrected errors you should audio-type it again. I began dictating Task four three at . . . .

End of Unit Four

Unit Five

I am now going to dictate some more paragraphs. You are going to start using the comma, so before you begin you should carefully study Reference Section Three in your book. Then look at the notes to Task five one. Are you now ready?

(POINT ON INDEX IS . . .)

Thank you for your recent letter enclosing your order for cottons, silks and woollen fabrics. **(full stop)** Unfortunately, we are out of stock of the cottons you require but our Purchasing Manager, Mr A North, expects delivery / next week. ½ **(paragraph)**

Referring to your previous order, the goods were despatched by fast, reliable, delivery van. **(full stop)** Please confirm in writing whether this method of delivery is satisfactory. **(full stop)** If there are problems, we shall do our // best to solve 1 them. **(paragraph)**

Mr John Jackson, our representative for the North West Area, will call to see you within the next week. **(full stop)** We hope you will place orders for nylon, rayon, terylene and other / synthetics for your summer styles. ½

(PAUSE)

Check your work from Model Task five one in your book. If you have made more than two uncorrected errors, you should audio-type it again. I began dictating Task five one at . . . .

I shall now dictate three more paragraphs. This is Task five two. Are you ready?

(POINT ON INDEX IS . . .)

The **(initial capitals)** Financial Director of our **(initial capital)** Company, Mrs Janice Roberts, started with the firm as a secretary. **(full stop)** She was eventually promoted to **(initial capitals)** Personal Assistant to the Managing Director. **(full stop)** She studied accountancy at evening classes, passing her / examinations in record time. **(full stop)** Mrs Roberts then ½ took up the post of Accounts Manager in 1981, and was eventually invited to be the Financial Director on the retirement of Mr James Gordon. **(paragraph)**

Mrs Roberts // is an excellent example to other women in the 1 Company who wish to progress from secretarial work to management posts. **(paragraph)**

When interviewed by the local newspaper, Mrs Roberts said that the hard work had been / worthwhile. **(full stop)** The most ½ difficult time, she agreed, was when her son, now three years old, was a tiny baby. **(full stop)** She said it was important that those women who desired to succeed in their chosen careers // 2 were firmly established in their jobs before taking time off to start a family.

(PAUSE)

Check your work from Model Task five two in your book. If you have made more than two uncorrected errors, you should audio-type it again. I began dictating Task five two at . . . .

I shall now dictate another three paragraphs for you to type. This is Production Task E for your teacher to mark. Make a note of the time and don't forget your name and the Task Number. Are you ready?

(POINT ON INDEX IS . . .)

Computers are becoming cheaper. **(full stop)** In fact a small home computer is very powerful when compared with its predecessors only ten years ago. **(full stop)** Personal computers can now do the tasks which previously would have needed computers / big enough to fill an entire room, costing ½ thousands of pounds, and needing several highly trained operators. **(paragraph)**

We are only at the beginning of the computer revolution. **(full stop)** We can expect more and more areas of // our lives to be 1 affected by computer use. **(full stop)** Usually the changes arrive without much fuss, and often without us even realizing that major changes in technology have happened. **(full stop)** In the past two decades we have / grown used to pocket ½ calculators, cashpoint machines at the banks, information systems linked to our televisions, and visual display units everywhere. **(paragraph)**

An expert on computer development, Mrs Jane Windsor, has predicted that computers will eventually // affect all aspects of 2 our lives by the end of the century. **(full stop)** Mr Brian Green, a computer consultant to many major companies, believes that the UK will continue to play a leading world role / in the ½ development of software.

(PAUSE)

Check your work for typing errors before handing it to your teacher for marking.

I shall now dictate another three paragraphs for you to type. This is Task five three. Are you ready?

(POINT ON INDEX IS . . .)

It is true that Christmas comes only once a year, but many businesses depend upon this one important day. **(full stop)** In the few weeks before Christmas, many manufacturers achieve as much as half of their total / sales. **(full stop)** This is true of ½ greeting card manufacturers, manufacturers of novelties and decorations, and even some food producers. **(full stop)** Christmas, despite what many people would rather believe, really is big business. **(paragraph)**

In fact, Christmas existed in // the form of a winter feast long before the religion which now gives it a name. **(full stop)** All European societies, it seems, felt the need for a cheerful holiday in the middle of the long, dark, / cold winter days. **(paragraph)** ½ **1**

So businessmen should not feel too guilty if the true spirit of Christmas sometimes seems to be lacking from their activities. **(full stop)** Mr Roy Charles, a **(initial capital)** Director of a famous London store, told // businessmen at a conference **2**

recently that they should keep up the good work of meeting the needs and wishes of the consumer at Christmas. **(full stop)** Many jobs, in addition to much happiness, depend on it. **(full stop)** / ½

Check your work from Task five three in your book. I began dictating that task at . . . .

End of Unit Five

Unit Six

By now you have covered some of the major work in your training as an audio-typist. I shall now dictate a short letter, but before typing it you should study Reference Section 4. When you are sure of letter display, turn to the notes to Task six one in your book, where you will find the address, reference, etc. Ready?

(POINT ON INDEX IS . . .)

Dear Mrs. Thompson,
Thank you for your recent enquiry about a portable typewriter for your own use. **(full stop)** We have several excellent models in stock, including electronic machines. **(full stop)** We suggest you call in at our shop / to inspect the full range. **½** **(paragraph)**

During next month this **(initial capital)** Branch will be holding its annual sale. **(full stop)** If you do not require the typewriter urgently, it would be to your advantage to wait. **(full stop)** The prices of // current models will be drastically reduced. **(full** **1** **stop)** Since you have placed orders with us in the past, we should like you to have the benefit of a price reduction.

> Yours sincerely,
> Michael Woods,
> Manager

(PAUSE)

Check your work from Model Task six one in your book. If you have made more than two uncorrected errors, you should audio-type it again. I began dictating at . . . .
I shall now dictate another letter, but first look at the notes to Task six two in your book. This letter has a heading, which will be dictated. Ready?

(POINT ON INDEX IS . . .)

Dear Sir,
(heading) MEMBERSHIP OF THE SOCIETY
In response to your recent request, I enclose a booklet which gives details of **(initial capital)** Membership of the **(initial capital)** Society, together with an application form. **(full stop)** When you have completed the form / you should return it to **½** me, enclosing the registration fee. **(paragraph)**

If you do not possess the necessary educational qualifications, you will be able to sit an entry examination next July. **(full** **stop)** Your attention is drawn to // the **(initial capitals)** **1** Examination Rules in the booklet. **(paragraph)**

I look forward to hearing further from you.
> Yours faithfully,
> Secretary

(PAUSE)

Check your work from Model Task six two in your book. I hope you used today's date. Also, did you remember to show that there were enclosures with the letter? These things are not dictated to you but are extremely important. I began dictating that letter at . . . so go back to that point and audio-type it again, if you made more than two errors.
I shall now dictate another short letter. This is Production Task F and it should be typed once only. Make sure your name is at the top of the paper and remember to time yourself. You will find the necessary information in the notes to Production Task F. Ready?

(POINT ON INDEX IS . . .)

Dear Sirs,
(heading) AGENCY SERVICES
We have pleasure in announcing details of our new **(initial capitals)** Copying Service. **(full stop)** We have a full range of equipment for printing, offset duplicating and photocopying. **(full stop)** Our charges are very reasonable, as you / will see **½** from the enclosed price list. **(paragraph)**

May we remind you that we continue to offer our services as an **(initial capitals)** Employment Agency for both your permanent and temporary staff requirements. **(full stop)** With the present shortage of // trained staff, you may have difficulties in **1** recruiting suitable people. **(full stop)** If so, we invite you to contact the **(initial capital)** Manager, Mrs. Short, who will be pleased to help you.

> Yours faithfully,
> OFFICE PERSONNEL LIMITED,
> K.A. / Bond, **½**
> Director

(PAUSE)

Carefully read through your work before taking it out of your machine and handing it to your teacher for marking. Don't forget to note the time you took.
I shall now dictate another short letter. This is Task six three. Are you ready?

(POINT ON INDEX IS . . .)

Dear Mr and Mrs Piper,
Thank you for your completed **(initial capitals)** Mortgage Application Form. **(full stop)** I am pleased to say that an advance will be made during the next few weeks. **(paragraph)**

We have written to your / solicitor today confirming that the mortgage application was successful. **(full stop)** We have asked her to let us know the date of **(initial capitals)** Exchange of Contracts as soon as possible, so that the overdraft facility to cover the // deposit can be made available. **(paragraph)**

We are now enclosing life assurance application forms for you both to complete and return.

    Yours sincerely
    Manager

½ **(PAUSE)**

 Check your work from Model Task six three in your book. I began dictating Task six three at . . . .

1

End of Unit Six

Unit Seven

I am now going to dictate a longer letter which will include some new instructions, so before beginning to type you should study Reference Section 5, which sets out the RSA dictating conventions, used in examinations. After you have studied Reference Section 5, look at the notes to Task seven one for the address, reference, etc. Are you now ready?

(POINT ON INDEX IS . . .)

Dear Mrs. Small,
I am writing to confirm our telephone conversation this morning and the arrangements for the visit to the Houses of Parliament by a party of our students on Thursday next. **(full stop)** These students / are studying government in connection with their ½ course in business studies. **(full stop)** As mentioned, they should arrive at fourteen thirty hours: **(colon)** there will be forty students and two lecturers. **(full stop)** It is really very kind of you // to conduct the tour personally, and I am sure the after- 1 noon will be both interesting and enjoyable. **(paragraph)**

May I call on your help in another way? **(question mark)** The **(initial capital)** College is taking as its theme for **(initial capitals)** Open / Day next term **(open single quotes, initial** ½ **capitals)** 'European Britain' **(close quotes)** and the idea behind this is to show the effects of **(initial capitals)** Common Market membership on British life. **(full stop)** As I know that you are very interested in the **(capital letters)** EEC, // I wonder 2 whether you would come and talk to our students on a topic related to this theme. **(full stop)** The date of Open Day could be arranged to suit your convenience, since you would be the / ½ main guest speaker. **(paragraph)**

I look forward to hearing from you and should like to thank you for the interest you show in the College.

Yours sincerely,
David Kennedy,
Principal

(PAUSE)

Check your work from Model Task seven one in your book. Did you manage to follow the new instructions correctly? If not, you should revise Reference Section 5. If you made more than two uncorrected errors, audio-type the letter again. I began dictating at . . . .
I shall now dictate another long letter for you to type. Look in your book for the notes to Task seven two. You will see that several new conventions will be introduced. Are you ready for Task seven two?

(POINT ON INDEX IS . . .)

Dear Sir,
(heading) SUPER WASHING MACHINE MODEL NUMBER THIRTY-ONE
I purchased one of your washing machines one month ago from the department store here in Ramsgate. **(full stop)** Since then it has given considerable trouble. **(paragraph)**

The / first time the machine was used it operated perfectly. ½ **(full stop)** However, the second time it was used, water flood-ed all over the floor. **(full stop)** I telephoned your office and was told that one of your repairmen // would call the next after- 1 noon — **(dash)** he did not. **(full stop)** He did, however, call the following morning when we were out. **(full stop)** My wife made two subsequent appointments for the repairman to call and was let down / on both occasions. **(full stop)** Eventually, ½ when he did keep the appointment, the repairman found that the machine needed a minor part which he did not have with him. **(full stop)** The part was fitted only yesterday, after // yet 2 another broken appointment. **(paragraph)**

I really must complain about this lack of service. **(full stop)** I believed that I was buying a machine from a firm with a first-**(hyphen)** class service; **(semi-colon)** unfortunately, this was not true. **(full stop)** I should / appreciate your comments. ½

Yours faithfully,
Robert Grant

(PAUSE)

Check your work from Model Task seven two in your book. I began dictating that task at . . . .
I shall now dictate another letter. You will find the relevant instructions in the notes to Task seven three in your book. Ready?

(POINT ON INDEX IS . . .)

Dear Sirs,
(heading) ORDER NUMBER B. **(stop)** two four nine
We have received your recent letter complaining about the poor condition of the china and crockery items which we delivered to you recently. **(full stop)** We have investigated the / matter and found that the order form which we received from ½ you had not been completed correctly. **(paragraph)**

The form states that you should **(open single quotes, initial capital)** 'Indicate the method of delivery by striking through two of the following: // **(colon)** road/ **(oblique)** rail/**(oblique)** 1 delivery van'. **(close quotes, full stop)** As your order was fragile, we think it should have been sent by delivery van. **(full stop)** You will note that in the **(initial capital)** Conditions printed on the reverse side of the order form, / it is clearly ½ stated that our **(initial capital)** Company cannot be held liable for breakages of fragile items in transit, unless **(underscore unless)** the goods are despatched by delivery van. **(full stop)** Unfortunately, whoever filled in the order form in your // office, asked for delivery by rail. **(paragraph)**

In the circumstances, therefore, we regret that we are unable to compensate you for the broken and cracked items.

Yours faithfully,
HOUSEHOLD PRODUCTS LIMITED
P. (for Peter) L. Jones

(PAUSE)

Check your work from Model Task seven three in your book. I began dictating that task at . . . .

The next letter is Production Task G and it should be typed once only. Make sure your name is on the top of the paper, and remember to time yourself. You will find all the necessary information in the notes to Production Task G. Ready?

(POINT ON INDEX IS . . .)

Dear Miss Jeffries,
Thank you for attending the interview here yesterday. **(full stop)** I am very pleased to confirm that I can offer you the position of secretary to the **(initial capitals)** Deputy Manager. **(full stop)** The hours of work are / oh nine thirty to seventeen

hundred hours from Monday to Friday: **(colon)** one hour is allowed for lunch. **(paragraph)**

I confirm that your annual salary will be **(words)** eight thousand pounds, plus luncheon vouchers of **(words)** seventy-five pence // per day. **(full stop)** You will be allowed to take annual holidays of four weeks altogether **(open brackets)** (but not more than two weeks may be taken consecutively). **(close brackets, paragraph)**

Would you please report direct to Mr. Rostron / (R O S T R O N) at ten hundred hours next Monday morning. **(full stop)** Please bring with you your tax documents. **(paragraph)**

I enclose a cheque for **(pound sign)** two point ten for your travelling expenses in connection // with the interview. **(full stop)** I look forward to working with you, and hope that you will let me know immediately if at any time you have problems connected with your employment.

Yours sincerely,
Personnel Manager /

(PAUSE)

Carefully re-check your work before handing it in to your teacher for marking. Don't forget to write on the bottom the time you took.

End of Unit Seven

Unit Eight

I shall now dictate a short memo. Before you start to type I should like you to look at Reference Section 6 in your book on memo display. When you are ready to start Task eight one look at the notes in your book. Ready?

(POINT ON INDEX IS . . .)

MEMO
To   Sales Manager
From Accounts Manager
(heading) GRICE (G R I C E) AND SONS LIMITED
Would you please note that the above **(initial capital)** Company are now above their credit limit. **(full stop)** I have heard from several / business associates that this firm has been ½ having a very difficult time lately. **(full stop)** In the circumstances, I think no further orders should be accepted from them until the major part of their balance is cleared. // 1 **(paragraph)**

Since you have good contacts with this firm I should be grateful if you would write them a tactful letter.

(PAUSE)

Check your work from Model Task eight one in your book. Check the display as well as the content. If you made more then two uncorrected errors, audio-type it again. I began dictating at . . . .

I shall now dictate another memo which I should like you to type on a printed memo form, if this is available. This is Task eight two.

(POINT ON INDEX IS . . .)

MEMO
To   Manchester Branch
From Head Office, London
(heading) STATIONERY SUPPLIES
At a recent meeting here, it was decided that all stationery supplies are to be purchased from Office Suppliers Limited, since an exceptionally large discount / has been granted for ½ bulk quantities. **(paragraph)**

It is important that you conform with **(initial capital)** Company policy on this matter, as failure by any branch to order from Office Suppliers may result in the Company not purchasing // a 1 total quantity sufficient to obtain this discount. **(paragraph)**

It is understood that your own local supplier can quote prices below those of Office Suppliers, but in this case your raised costs will be offset by / savings at other branches throughout ½ the country. **(full stop)** Would you please ensure that all further orders for stationery are sent to: **(colon)** The Purchas-

ing Manager, Office Suppliers Limited, ten Green Lane, London, N4 8QQ. //

2

(PAUSE)

Check your work from Model Task eight two in your book. I began dictating at . . . .

The next memo is Production Task H. Make sure that your name is at the top of your paper. Remember, a production task should be typed once only and should be timed. Are you ready?

(POINT ON INDEX IS . . .)

MEMO
To   Company Secretary
From Sales Manager
(heading) GENERAL ENGINEERING LIMITED: **(colon)** ANNUAL DINNER
I confirm our telephone conversation of this morning and am attaching two complimentary tickets for the Annual Exhibition and Dinner of General / Engineering Limited at the Grand ½ Hotel, Kings Road. **(full stop)** As mentioned, I have an important last- **(hyphen)** minute engagement and cannot attend personally. **(paragraph)**

It should be a very pleasant evening, but I suggest you look through the appropriate // files before you go, in case anything 1 concerning business crops up. **(full stop)** My main contact with General Engineering is Mr. Robert Jenkinson, the Sales Director. **(full stop)** My secretary telephoned explaining that you will be coming in my / place. **(full stop)** Mr. Jenkinson ½ said that he would meet you at eight p.m. in the **(initial capitals)** Reception Area of the Hotel.

(PAUSE)

Re-check your work before handing it to your teacher to mark. Remember to note on the bottom how many minutes you took.

I shall now dictate a short letter. Before you start to type, I should like you to study Reference Section 7 on Indexing. Having studied this section carefully, look at the notes to Task eight three. You must decide what size paper and margins you should use. Are you now ready for Task eight three?

(POINT ON INDEX IS . . .)

Dear Sir,
(heading) ACCOUNT NUMBER three one seven nine nine
It is with regret that we must draw your attention to the fact that your account with our **(initial capital)** Company is now considerably overdue. **(paragraph)**

Under the terms / of the **(initial capital)** Agreement, you ½
guaranteed to pay **(pound sign)** fifteen point thirty-one per
month, or ten per cent of the outstanding balance — **(dash)**
whichever figure is the smaller. **(full stop)** Your arrears now
total **(pound sign)** forty-five point ninety-three. **(full stop)** We
should appreciate // payment by return of post.   1

> Yours faithfully,
> REGAL STORES LIMITED,
> Accounts Manager

(PAUSE)

    Check your work from Model Task eight three in your book.
If you have made more than two uncorrected errors, you
should audio-type it again. I began dictating at . . . .
    I shall now dictate a long memo. This is Task eight four.
Ready?

(POINT ON INDEX IS . . .)

MEMO
To   General Manager
From Staff Manager
(heading) CAR PARKING
I am writing to you to report on the meeting with the **(initial
capitals)** Works Committee yesterday evening, in view of the
fact that I am going on / holiday tomorrow, and have been ½
unable to contact you all the afternoon. **(paragraph)**

The main problem that was discussed was the question of car
parking. **(full stop)** Whilst it is appreciated that parking space
at the factory // is somewhat limited, the shop- **(hyphen)** floor   1
workers complained about the system by which spaces are
allocated. **(full stop)** They accept that all senior managers
should have reserved places in the car park, but they want the
remaining spaces / given out on a different basis than at ½
present. **(full stop)** At the moment spaces are awarded on the
basis of seniority in the Company. **(full stop)** However, in
practice, this has meant that office staff have had priority //   2
over shop-floor workers. **(full stop)** It was felt by most workers
present that there was no justification for allocating a space to
every new manager or secretary, rather than to a long-
(hyphen) serving production worker. **(full stop)** It was suggested, / therefore, that spaces be allocated on the basis of ½
years of service with the Company. **(paragraph)**

Something must be done fairly soon as there is a strong feeling
of resentment because some new, young typists have // been   3
given spaces recently. **(paragraph)**

My own feeling is that we should get the new car park ready
earlier than originally planned and, in the meantime, adopt the
scheme proposed by the production workers for any / further ½
allocations. **(paragraph)**

I shall be back in the office on Monday fortnight.

(PAUSE)

    Check your work from Model Task eight four in your book. I
began dictating that memo at . . ., so if you need to audio-
type it again, go back to that point.
    I am now going to dictate a letter to Mr. Kimpton. This is
Task eight five. Ready?

(POINT ON INDEX IS . . .)

Dear Mr. Kimpton,
Thank you for your recent letter. **(full stop)** I enclose the
(capital letters) BA and British Caledonian timetables you
requested. **(full stop)** Both airlines have flights to Spain.
(paragraph)

I have investigated your complaint about the service on / board ½
a recent flight from Tangier (T A N G I E R) to London. **(full
stop)** The **(initial capitals)** Public Relations Officer for the
airline states that the flight on which you travelled home
should have called at // Gibraltar on the way to Tangier. **(full   1
stop)** However, the plane could not land at Gibraltar because
of gale force winds: **(colon)** the runway there is very short.
(full stop) Thus the fresh food and drinks ordered there were
not, / of course, taken on board, and the **(initial capitals)** ½
Chief Stewardess had to get emergency supplies at Tangier.
(full stop) These supplies were not up to the usual high stan-
dards of the airline. **(paragraph)**

I trust this explanation is acceptable // and look forward to   2
receiving your booking for your forthcoming trip to Spain.
> Yours sincerely,
> John Hopkins,
> Manager

(PAUSE)

    Check your work from Model Task eight five in your book. I
began dictating at . . . .

End of Unit Eight

Unit Nine

I shall now dictate a short report, but before you begin to type you must study Reference Section 8 which deals with the use of the apostrophe. After you have done this you should turn to the notes to Task nine one before starting to type. This passage contains a number of apostrophes, so be careful. Ready?

(POINT ON INDEX IS . . .)

(centred heading, closed capitals, underscored) JOHN CONSTABLE AND COMPANY LIMITED
The **(initial capitals)** Company's Annual General Meeting was held at the offices in Green Street, Glasgow, on twenty-first March. **(full stop)** The **(initial capital)** Chairman's statement had been previously circulated. **(paragraph)**

The year's results were fairly good / considering strong com- ½ petition from abroad. **(full stop)** Some new lines had to be sold at uneconomic prices, and this did not help the Company's profits. **(full stop)** Many companies' accounts showed decreased dividends similar to Constable's. **(full stop)** The Chairman remarked // that an encouraging fact was that competitors' **1** results were less satisfactory. **(paragraph)**

The Chairman thanked the **(initial capital)** Directors for their hard work and pointed out that they depend to a large extent on the staff's loyalty. **(full stop)** A / vote of thanks was proposed ½ by one of the shareholders and unanimously approved.

(PAUSE)

Check your work from Model Task nine one, paying particular attention to the apostrophes. If you have made more than two mistakes you should revise Reference Section 8 again and then audio-type another attempt. I began dictating at . . . .
I shall now dictate a memo which also contains a number of words with apostrophes. This is Task nine two. Ready?

(POINT ON INDEX IS . . .)

MEMO
To   All Departmental Managers
From Personnel Manager
(heading) CONDITIONS OF SERVICE
You are reminded of the following points concerning the above: **(colon. Typist, there now follow five numbered items)**
One   The hours of work at the **(initial capital)** Company's offices are nine am to / five pm. **(full stop)** The hours of work ½ at the Company's factories are eight am to five thirty pm. **(next item)**

Two   Directors, managers and employees with three years' **1** experience of working for the Company are // entitled to contribute to the **(initial capitals)** Pension Fund. **(next item)**

Three   All employees of the Company are entitled to three weeks' annual holiday: **(colon)** employees who have worked for five years qualify for an extra week's holiday. **(next item)**

Four   Company / cars are provided for all managers. **(full** ½ **stop)** The firm's cars are not to be used for any individual's private business. **(full stop)** Directors' cars may be parked in the reserved car park. **(next item)**

Five   It is each manager's responsibility // to ensure his staff **2** arrive punctually, and to report any employee's absence.

(PAUSE)

Check your work from Model Task nine two in your book. If you have made more than one error connected with the apostrophe, you should audio-type the memo again, without referring to your first attempt. I began dictating at . . . .
The next task is a production task for your teacher to mark. Make sure that your name and Production Task I appear at the top of your paper, and time yourself. You must type this task once only. This is a letter and you will find the address in the notes to Production Task I. Ready?

(POINT ON INDEX IS . . .)

Dear Miss Bolch,
Thank you for your letter of yesterday's date, enclosing your order. **(full stop)** Unfortunately, we no longer manufacture the range of women's swimsuits you require. **(full stop)** The models you have chosen are from last year's / catalogue. ½ **(paragraph)**

We are enclosing our new catalogue, which shows our Company's latest designs. **(full stop)** We are sure you will agree that we have an excellent range, and that you will find some suitable styles. **(full stop)** You can // order direct from us, **1** enclosing your firm's cheque for the appropriate amount, or you can ask our **(initial capital)** Representative to call on you. **(full stop)** Our Representative's name is Mr. Robert James, and the Company's telephone number is / given above. **(full** ½ **stop)** He will be very pleased to hear from you.

Yours sincerely,
Sales Manager

(PAUSE)

Carefully re-check your work before handing it in to your teacher for marking. Pay attention to the use of apostrophes.
I am now going to dictate a letter which contains a number of similarly sounding words, so that you have to think about the spelling and meaning of the words. Study Reference Section

9. When you have done this, you can look at the notes to Task nine three for details of the next letter. This letter is quite difficult, so be careful. Ready?

(POINT ON INDEX IS . . .)

Dear Mrs Josephs,
I am pleased to say that your case will come before the **(initial capital)** Court within the next few weeks. **(full stop)** The correspondence has already been forwarded to the **(initial capitals)** Queen's Counsel, who will advise on / the main ½ points of law. **(full stop)** He will study the draft document, which states the principles raised by the case. **(full stop)** The **(capital letters)** Q. **(stop)** C. **(stop)** will then send us his opinion, trying to elicit the main points of // disagreement in the 1 dispute. **(paragraph)**

I enclose a draft letter to the defendant for you to check, which states our principal objections to his claims. **(full stop)** When you have had the opportunity to study the draft, please / en- ½ sure that you return it to me as soon as possible. **(full stop)** We shall see what effect this has! **(exclamation mark)**

Yours sincerely,

(PAUSE)

Check your work from Model Task nine three in your book. That was tricky, so don't worry if your first attempt was not very good. If you made more than two errors you should audio-type the task again, without referring to your previous work. I began dictating at . . . .
I shall now dictate a memo testing more of the similar-sounding words listed in Reference Section 9. This is Task nine four. Ready?

(POINT ON INDEX IS . . .)

MEMO
To   Foreman
From Site Manager
(heading) KING STREET SITE
Would you please note that work on the new site will commence next Monday morning, weather permitting. **(full stop)** The licence has now been received from the town / council. ½ **(full stop)** Would you please hire four additional labourers for this important job. **(paragraph)**

We are very short of both lead pipes and steel tubes, and will need to take delivery of a further supply as soon // as possible. 1

(full stop) The last load was left under canvas on the site and has disappeared. **(full stop)** The police advise us to make better arrangements to ensure we do not lose it this time — **(dash)** there are many / people who will steal lead for its value ½ sold as scrap. **(full stop)** Unfortunately, we are unable to insure ourselves against this type of loss.

(PAUSE)

Carefully check your work from Model Task nine four in your book. I began dictating at . . . .
The next task is a production task for your teacher to mark. Make sure that your name and "Production Task J" appear at the top of your paper and don't forget to time yourself. This task, which is a short report, should be typed once only. Are you now ready for Production Task J?

(POINT ON INDEX IS . . .)

(heading, capitals, underscored) SHORTAGE OF SECRETARIAL STAFF
Britain's export trade is being affected by a shortage of trained secretaries. **(full stop)** The **(initial capitals)** Assistant Director of the **(initial capitals)** Export Council for Britain said that most companies were experiencing difficulty in obtaining good / bi-lingual secretaries. **(full stop)** In the past, it was not ½ difficult to hire suitable staff to meet their needs. **(full stop)** The principal reason for the shortage is that far more opportunities exist for intelligent women nowadays: **(colon)** there // 1 are a larger number of careers from which to choose. **(paragraph)**

To ensure a larger supply of good secretaries, salaries will have to be a good deal higher than formerly. **(full stop)** Career opportunities within the business world / will also have to be ½ widened. **(full stop)** This will enable the more capable women to set their sights on managerial jobs. **(full stop)** If nothing is done to raise the promotion prospects of women entering their employment, commercial // organizations will lose the best 2 workers to other professions.

(PAUSE)

When you have checked your work carefully, hand it to your teacher for marking.

End of Unit Nine

Unit Ten

I shall now dictate a draft letter. Before you start typing, look at the notes to Task ten one in your book. Ready?

(POINT ON INDEX IS . . .)

Dear Mr Wilson,
(heading) ABRAHAM AND COMPANY LIMITED
Further to your recent letter, we have made the necessary enquiries concerning the above company. **(full stop)** The partners in the business are Mr. S. **(for Samuel)** Abraham and Mr. R. Rice. / **(full stop)** The company manufactures leather goods ½ on a small scale and sells direct to retail outlets. **(full stop)** Mr. Rice has a record of business failure — **(dash)** a company which he managed and owned went bankrupt seven years ago. // **(full stop)** It appears that one of his partners was taking 1 too much cash out of the business and eventually had to serve a term in prison. **(full stop)** Obviously, this failure was due mainly to circumstances beyond the / control of Mr. Rice. **(full ½ stop)** Our informants tell us that the personal reputation of Mr. Rice is sound. **(paragraph)**

However, in the circumstances, it may be best to be cautious. **(full stop)** We suggest that at least the first // few orders be 2 accepted on a cash- **(hyphen)** with- **(hyphen)** order basis. **(full stop)** If you subsequently decide to grant a credit limit to this company, we think it should be at the minimum level consistent with the maintenance / of good business relationships. ½ **(paragraph)**

We trust the above information is of service to you, and assure you of our strictest confidence.

        Yours sincerely,

(PAUSE)

    Check your work from Model Task ten one in your book. I began dictating that task at . . . so if you need to audio-type it again, go back to that point.
    I shall now dictate a circular letter, details of which are given in the notes to Task ten two in your book. Ready?

(POINT ON INDEX IS . . .)

Dear Sir/ **(oblique)** Madam,
You will be interested to hear that we have recently brought out a new range of cosmetics which we are sure you will want to market. **(full stop)** This complete range of beauty products / is designed for the thirteen to nineteen age group and is ½ attractively packaged in bright yellow containers. **(full stop)** We are enclosing fully descriptive literature and a price list. **(paragraph)**

Our **(initial capital)** Representative will call on you in the // 1 very near future to deliver a special display cabinet for use with these products. **(full stop)** As an introductory offer, we will allow a twenty per cent discount on goods purchased within the next three months. **(paragraph)**

We / look forward to receiving your order in the near future. ½

        Yours faithfully
        SUSAN SMITH PRODUCTS
        Sales Manager

(PAUSE)

    Check your work from Model Task ten two in your book. I began dictating at . . . .
    I shall now dictate a draft circular letter which is to be displayed as it will look when duplicated. This is Production Task K and it should be typed once only and timed. Are you ready?

(POINT ON INDEX IS . . .)

Dear Madam,
(heading) SUMMER SALES CAMPAIGN
Thank you for your recent application to join our team of sales demonstration staff for our **(figure)** third national sales campaign. **(full stop)** We should like you to attend for interview at the / following address and time: **(colon. Typist please leave ½ one clear inch for insertion of details) (paragraph)**

If you are recruited to the team you will be required to wear our smart, fashionable suit at all times when on **(initial capital)** Company business. **(full stop)** You will be provided with a white // Ford Escort car and, in this connection, should bring 1 your driving licence to the interview. **(full stop)** You must be prepared to travel extensively throughout the campaign and to work overtime if required. **(full stop)** Would you please confirm / whether you will attend the interview at the time stated ½ above.

        Yours faithfully
        PRESIDENT CIGARETTE COMPANY
        LIMITED
        John Austin,
        Sales Manager

(PAUSE)

    Make sure your name and "Production Task K" are on the paper before handing it in for marking. Note the time you took.

I shall now dictate a Staff Notice for you to type. This is Task ten three. Are you ready?

(POINT ON INDEX IS . . .)

(heading, closed capitals) STAFF NOTICE
(side heading, initial capitals, underscored) Coffee and Tea Breaks
The canteen is becoming very crowded each morning at approximately **(words)** eleven o'clock and long queues have been forming at the counters. **(full stop)** It would be of considerable help if staff / could try to stagger their breaks over a ½ longer period, and avoid crowding in the middle of the morning. **(paragraph)**

It has also been noticed that some staff are taking considerably longer than the fifteen minutes // allowed for tea and coffee 1 breaks. **(full stop)** Because some staff are sitting at tables too long, others arriving later cannot find seats in the canteen. **(full stop)** Please leave the canteen after fifteen minutes to avoid causing this / congestion. **(paragraph)** ½

It is hoped that staff will voluntarily take action to reduce pressure on the canteen facilities. **(full stop)** If there is no improvement, however, management will have to take steps to ensure that breaks are more // strictly regulated. 2

STAFF MANAGER

(PAUSE)

Check your work from Model Task ten three in your book. I began dictating that task at . . . .

I shall now dictate an article which is Task ten four in your book. Are you ready?

(POINT ON INDEX IS . . .)

(centred heading, capital letters) COMMUNITY ARTS FESTIVAL
The **(initial capitals)** Community Arts Festival in **(initial capital)** East London was the scene last week of a variety of activities, reflecting the great richness of the many cultures of people in this multi- **(hyphen)** ethnic community. / **(paragraph)** ½

Among the events featured was a beautiful display of traditional dances performed by members of the Asian communities, when the wonderful colours and fabrics of costumes were also much admired. **(paragraph)**

The West Indian community organized // a lively carnival, 1 accompanied by the music of steel bands. **(full stop)** Everyone joined in this with much enthusiasm. **(paragraph)**

English cultural tradition was represented by a range of traditional and modern plays at the local theatre. **(full stop)** Highlight of / the week was the party to which each ethnic group ½ contributed typical food and delicacies.

(PAUSE)

Check your work from Model Task ten four in your book. I began dictating at . . . .

End of Unit Ten

Unit Eleven

RSA AUDIO-TYPEWRITING, STAGE 1, MARCH 1983

Before each passage you will be told its length and the title or addressee. Further instructions may also be dictated before the passage begins, but before you start typing make sure that you have read the instructions on the printed paper handed to you by the Invigilator. Addresses and references not given in the dictation are printed on that paper.

Passage 1 – A circular letter of 182 words

Minutes

Dear Sir/ **(oblique)** Madam
Everyone interested in books is aware that prices are very high. **(full stop)** Many people would like to own more books but cannot afford to buy them because of the increased cost of living. / **(paragraph)**   ½

We have decided to offer, at bargain prices, a number of recently published books and a selection from previous lists. **(full stop)** A copy of our sale catalogue is enclosed. **(full stop)** This offer is open until the end // of July nineteen eighty-three   1
and applies only to the United Kingdom. **(full stop)** Payment can be made by cheque, **(initial capitals)** National Giro, Barclaycard or Access. **(full stop)** If your order comes to more than **(pound sign)** twenty, you may choose / a book from the   ½
free gift page. **(paragraph)**

A word of warning! **(exclamation mark)** Some of the titles offered are in limited supply. **(full stop)** If there is one which you would particularly like to own, please send for it // im-   2
mediately – **(dash)** you may be disappointed if you delay. **(paragraph)**

We hope that you will benefit from our sale. **(full stop)** Should you know of anyone else who would be interested in our offer, please ask them to write / to us for a catalogue.   ½

Yours truly

Passage 2 – A notice of 112 words

Minutes

The aim of the safety year is to reduce the high level of accidents in the **(initial capitals)** Construction Industry. **(full stop)** Many workers take unnecessary risks. **(full stop)** Most accidents that happen could, and should, be prevented. **(paragraph)**

A safety exhibition, / open from ten a m until eight p m, will be   ½
held at the **(initial capitals)** Technical College on Wednesday, Thursday and Friday of next week. **(full stop)** Admission will be free. **(paragraph)**

The directors of our firm wish all // employees to visit the   1
exhibition and particularly to see the excellent training films

which will run continuously. **(full stop)** Arrangements have been made for everyone to go during working hours **(open brackets)** (without loss of pay). **(close brackets, full stop)** Your supervisor will / tell you when your coach will leave.   ½

Passage 3 – A letter of 147 words to Henderson & James Ltd

Minutes

Dear Sirs
On fifteenth June, Clarke Limited, the well- **(hyphen)** known office equipment firm, will open an extension to their London showrooms. **(full stop)** In that week's issue of our newspaper we shall include a special article contained / in a   ½
four-**(hyphen)** page supplement announcing this important event. **(paragraph)**

We understand that you have supplied them with office sundries for many years. **(full stop)** You are invited to insert in this supplement an advertisement linking your firm // and its   1
products with Clarke Limited. **(full stop)** We are offering a discount of twenty per cent off our usual charges. **(paragraph)**

Over the last two years we have printed several of these supplements. **(full stop)** Most firms who have / taken up our   ½
offer say that they consider improvements in their sales were largely due to this particular form of advertising. **(paragraph)**

Some samples of advertisements **(open brackets)** (with prices) **(close brackets)** and an order form are enclosed. **(full stop)** Please telephone // if you require further information.   2

Yours faithfully

Passage 4 – A memorandum of 119 words to Managing Director

Minutes

Our new offices will be ready by late November. **(full stop)** We had thought that we could manage with the space available until then. **(full stop)** However, our business is expanding so quickly that we must have more room / now. **(paragraph)**   ½

We could easily stand a portable cabin against the west wall of the office block. **(full stop)** The audio- **(hyphen)** typists could occupy it; **(semi-colon)** their present accommodation could be used by the accounts department. **(paragraph)**

Hiring a cabin // would be better than buying – **(dash)** it would   1
be needed for only a few months. **(full stop)** The cost would be the hiring charge less the tax saved. **(paragraph)**

Some illustrated brochures are attached; **(semi-colon)** I have marked the cabin / which I consider would be most suitable.   ½
(full stop) Please let me have your comments soon.

End of Unit Eleven

Unit Twelve

RSA AUDIO-TYPEWRITING, STAGE 1, MAY 1984

Before each passage you will be told its length and the title or addressee. Further instructions may also be dictated before the passage begins, but before you start typing make sure that you have read the instructions on the printed paper handed to you by the Invigilator. Addresses and references not given in the dictation are printed on that paper.

Passage 1 — A letter of 194 words
Minutes

Dear Miss Lawson
With reference to your interview at this office yesterday, I confirm that I am prepared to offer you the position of **(initial capitals)** Junior Clerical Assistant as from Monday, twenty-first May. **(full stop)** You will / be working for my **(initial** ½ **capitals)** Private Secretary, Miss Karen Green, whom you met yesterday. **(paragraph)**

As was pointed out at the interview, the starting salary **(open brackets)** (paid on a monthly basis) **(close brackets)** is **(pound sign)** four thousand, and annual increments // are **1** **(pound sign)** five hundred. **(full stop)** Luncheon vouchers are also given to all staff each week. **(paragraph)**

I am enclosing a booklet setting out the terms and conditions of service, and may I suggest that you read this / carefully and ½ keep it by you for future reference. **(paragraph)**

As was mentioned at the interview, I confirm that I will make arrangements for you to attend the local **(initial capitals)** College of Further Education on a day- **(hyphen)** // release basis, **2** to further your secretarial and business studies qualifications. **(full stop)** When you come to the office on the Monday morning, ask at the reception desk for Miss Green and she will come to meet you. / **(paragraph)** ½

We look forward to your joining the Company and hope that you will be happy with us.

Yours sincerely

Passage 2 — A memorandum of 112 words
Minutes

As you know, we appointed Sandra Lawson yesterday as your new assistant — **(dash)** she is starting on Monday, twenty-first May, and I said you would meet her at **(initial capital)** Reception when she arrives. **(paragraph)**

Please plan an / induction (I N D U C T I O N) programme for ½ Sandra, covering the first month of her employment with the Company, and also write to the local College of Further Education asking for particulars of day-release courses in secretarial

and business // studies. **(full stop)** She already has some basic **1** knowledge of micro- **(hyphen)** computers and word processors and has expressed a desire to study this field in more detail. **(full stop)** Please mention this in your letter to the College, as / ½ they run specialist courses in these subjects.

Passage 3 — An article of 179 words
Minutes

Many office buildings now have an open- **(hyphen)** plan layout in place of many smaller rooms enclosed by walls. **(full stop)** It is usual practice to divide such a large office into several smaller working areas, and plants / are an attractive way of ½ doing this. **(full stop)** Plants make such a difference to the appearance of rooms that contain only desks, chairs and filing cabinets — **(dash)** they help to create a pleasant working environment and // brighten up the room. **(full stop)** Plants are **1** especially effective in reception areas where they give a welcome and convey a sense of care and interest. **(paragraph)**

Care should be taken to position the plants so that they do / not ½ interfere with the movements of office personnel. **(full stop)** Therefore plants grouped together in varying heights make a more effective display than those placed individually. **(full stop)** Furthermore they grow better when grouped together, as the humidity (H U M I D I T Y) around // them is increased. **2** **(paragraph)**

Water used in either a small pool or a fountain may make an attractive feature when landscaping, and also provides the surrounding plants with moist air in which to grow, and this / is ½ better for them.

Passage 4 — A letter of 75 words to Mr D Edwards
Minutes

Dear Mr. Edwards
I confirm my telephone conversation with you this morning and set out below the arrangements we made regarding the landscaping of your open- **(hyphen)** plan offices. **(Typist, there now follow three numbered paragraphs)**

One. My staff will commence work at / eight a m on Friday next. ½ Two. The work will take approximately six hours to complete. Three. A florist will call each Friday morning to maintain the plants and shrubs. **(paragraph)**

Good luck with your new // micro- **(hyphen)** computing **1** venture.

Yours sincerely

End of Unit Twelve

Unit Thirteen

I am now going to dictate a circular letter of eighty-one words which has short dictated display in the middle. Before you start typing, look at the notes to Task thirteen one in your book.

(POINT ON INDEX IS . . .)

Dear Member,
This year's bonus offer of music cassettes in the classical section of the **(initial capital)** Club's list is the following three symphonies recently recorded by the London Festival Orchestra: **(colon)**

Beethoven Symphony Number 6 **(open single quotes)** 'Pastoral' **(close quotes)** Mozart Symphony Number thirty-eight **(open single quotes)** 'Prague' / **(close quotes)** Schubert ½ Symphony Number eight **(open single quotes)** 'Unfinished' **(close quotes) (paragraph)**

For this special bonus offer, cassettes are priced **(pound sign)** two point seven five each, or seven pounds for the set. **(full stop)** This offer is open until the end of next month, and the order form is enclosed. // 1

        Yours sincerely,
        CASSETTE MUSIC LIMITED

(PAUSE)

    Check your work from Model Task thirteen one in your book. If you feel you need to audio-type that task again, go back to . . . . .
    I am now going to dictate a letter of one hundred and thirty-seven words which has dictated display and a correction to be incorporated. Before you start typing, study the notes to Task thirteen two. Ready?

(POINT ON INDEX IS . . .)

Dear Mr Machin,
Further to your visit to our **(initial capital)** Agency yesterday when we discussed **(initial capitals)** Italian Tour Number seventy-eight in our brochure, we have pleasure in informing you that we have provisionally reserved the following accommodation for you: **(colon)**

Week beginning / eighteenth July — **(dash)** one double room ½ with bath at the Park Hotel in Rome
Week beginning twenty-fifth July — **(dash)** one twin-**(hyphen)** bedded room at the Hotel Maria in Naples. **(paragraph)**

We confirm that the price as advertised includes all travel from the **(initial capitals)** West London // Air Terminal to the first 1 hotel, between the hotels, and return. **(full stop)** If you wish to

secure this booking, a deposit of **(pound sign)** five pounds per person is required within the next ten days. **(full stop)** This can be paid by cheque or in / cash at the Agency. **(paragraph)** ½

I look forward to hearing further from you.

        Yours sincerely,
        John Martin,
        Manager

(PAUSE)

    Check your work from Model Task thirteen two in your book. It is not of course essential that you display the information about the hotels in exactly the same way as illustrated. Did you remember to incorporate the correction at the appropriate point? If you feel you need to audio-type Task thirteen two again, I began dictating at . . . .
    I shall now dictate a memo of one hundred and forty-six words which contains dictated display. This is Task thirteen three. The notes to this task should be read before you commence. Ready?

(POINT ON INDEX IS . . .)

MEMO
To   Staff
From Personnel Manager
(heading) ANNUAL DINNER AND DANCE
The **(initial capitals)** Annual Dinner and Dance will take place at the Swan Hotel on twelfth June at seven thirty p m. **(full stop)** Tickets will be available during the preceding fortnight, on sale / in the **(initial capitals)** Accounts Department. **(full ½ stop)** Tickets cost **(pound sign)** seven pounds double and four pounds single. **(full stop)** After discussion, the **(initial capitals)** Staff Committee selected the following simple menu, which it was felt would appeal to most people: **(colon. Typist, please display the following menu)**

Oxtail Soup or Chilled Melon **(next course)**
Roast Pork with // Stuffing or Grilled Lamb Cutlets 1
Roast and Creamed Potatoes
Cauliflower, Carrots and Green Beans **(next course)**
Fresh Fruit Salad and Cream or Sherry Trifle **(next course)**
Cheese and Biscuits **(next course)**
Coffee
(paragraph)

It is hoped that the dinner will prove to be as great a success / ½ as in previous years. **(full stop)** Dancing will be to the Latin Trio and a mobile discotheque. **(full stop)** The cabaret will include entertainment from the comedian, Eric Peters.

(PAUSE)

Check your work from Model Task thirteen three in your book. Did you remember to start each item of the meal on a new line, with double spacing between courses? I began dictating Task thirteen three at . . . .

I shall now dictate a memo of one hundred and sixty-five words which contains a dictated agenda. Make sure your name and "Production Task L" are at the top of your paper and time yourself. Look at the notes to Production Task L before starting.

(POINT ON INDEX IS . . .)

MEMO
To   Sales Manager, Accounts Manager, London Area
      Manager
From Managing Director
(heading) SALES MEETINGS
It was decided at a recent meeting of the **(initial capital)** Board that the Sales Department Manager should hold official sales meetings with the Accounts Department Manager on / a ½ regular basis, so that there is better liaison on matters relating to customers' accounts, credit limits, etc. Area Sales Managers may also be invited to attend if items affecting their specific areas are to be discussed. **(paragraph)**

Accordingly, would you // please arrange to attend the first of 1 these meetings to be held in the **(initial capitals)** Board Room next Wednesday at fourteen hundred hours. **(full stop)** The agenda will be as follows: **(colon)**
(heading, spaced capitals) AGENDA
one   Reports and matters arising
two   Analysis of new accounts
three / Discount rates for London Area ½
four   Credit limits in view of recent restrictions
five   Any other business
(paragraph)

Would you please prepare the appropriate reports for the first item on the agenda. **(full stop)** These meetings will be held on the first Wednesday // of each month, so please arrange your 2 appointments accordingly.

(PAUSE)

Make sure your name, "Production Task L", and the time you took are on your paper. Check your work carefully before handing it to your teacher. Mark up the copies ready for circulation.

I shall now dictate a letter of one hundred and sixty-three words which contains dictated display. This is Task thirteen four. Ready?

(POINT ON INDEX IS . . .)

Dear Sir,
Further to my visit to the block of flats at five to eight Gloucester Road, I have pleasure in quoting my **(initial capital)** Company's price for the interior decoration of the staircases and communal entrance halls, and for the painting / of the exterior woodwork. ½ **(full stop)** The quotation is as follows: **(colon. Typist, please set out the following information)**

Decoration of staircases and all external woodwork **(PAUSE)** **(pound sign)** two thousand two hundred pounds.
Replastering of water- **(hyphen)** damaged walls in main hall **(PAUSE)** one hundred and sixty pounds.
Painting of concrete sections between exterior brickwork // 1 **(open brackets)** if required **(close brackets)** **(PAUSE)** one hundred and ninety pounds.
Total **(pound sign)** three thousand five hundred pounds plus **(capital letters)** VAT at fifteen per cent.

I confirm that six men will be employed on this job and that the work can start in approximately / two months' time. **(full stop)** ½ If this quotation is acceptable, I shall deliver paint colour charts immediately so that the **(initial capitals)** Residents Committee may make their choice. **(full stop)** This will ensure that the paint is ordered and delivered well before the work is due // to 2 commence. **(paragraph)**

I assure you of our prompt and reliable attention at all times.

        Yours faithfully,
        RUGBY BUILDERS LIMITED
        John K. Rugby,
        Director.

(PAUSE)

Check your work from Model Task thirteen four in your book. I began dictating at . . . .

End of Unit Thirteen

Unit Fourteen

I am now going to dictate an article of two hundred and fifty-two words which is Task fourteen one. There is a table to accompany this passage. Are you ready?

(POINT ON INDEX IS . . .)

(centred heading, capitals, underscored) EXCEL GARAGE DOORS
EXCEL garage doors are made to measure garage doors. **(full stop)** There is therefore no need to adhere to standard opening sizes when building new garages. **(full stop)** Nor is there any necessity to convert an existing opening to a standard / door ½ size when replacing old doors. **(full stop)** EXCEL up-**(hyphen)** and- **(hyphen)** over doors are made to measure doors at the same prices as for standard doors. **(full stop)** They incorporate the best principles of overhead door design, and require the minimum of space and maintenance. **(paragraph)**

The // up-and-over door mechanism is of robust construction. **1** **(full stop)** The door is securely held in the raised position, yet is gently lowered at a touch. **(full stop)** There are several design specifications available. **(paragraph)**

The **(capital letters)** MODERN up-and-over door combines the best features of both aluminium / and steel. **(full stop)** The ½ welded steel frame is coated after assembly with a rustproofed zinc finish, suitable for painting. **(full stop)** It provides a sturdy framework that will withstand heavy and constant use. **(full stop)** The aluminium panels are strong, weather- **(hyphen)** resisting, and have an attractive // finish. **(full stop)** The **2** MODERN garage door is exceptionally good value and is the cheapest of our range. **(paragraph)**

(capital letters) TRADITIONAL up-and-over doors can be styled in either Georgian or Tudor design. **(full stop)** They are constructed of either black or white coloured glass fibre. **(full stop)** The / Tudor style door has a simulated wood grain finish. ½ **(paragraph)**

The **(capital letters)** COUNTRY up-and-over door is also made of glass fibre. **(full stop)** This has a wood grain finish but is designed in a way which will blend with any house style. **(paragraph)**

There is // no difference in the cost of TRADITIONAL and **3** COUNTRY up-and-over garage doors.

(PAUSE)

Check your work from Model Task fourteen one in your book. Carefully check the accompanying table. Your teacher will advise you whether or not you need to repeat this work. I began dictating at . . . .

I shall now dictate a letter which also contains a table of figures. The table to go with Task fourteen two is printed on page 19 of your book. Look at the notes to Task fourteen two for the address, etc.

(POINT ON INDEX IS . . .)

Dear Madam,
(heading) STATEMENT NUMBER J two three two two
Thank you for your recent letter. **(full stop)** In order to clarify the position for you I set out below details of the items shown on your statement for last month: **(colon. Typist, please display the list of book titles given in your book) (paragraph)**

It seems / that the confusion has arisen over the return of fifty ½ books by Bellamy and the purchase of fifty of a different title by the same author, but at a higher **(underscore higher)** price. **(paragraph)**

We trust that this clarifies the situation for you // and look **1** forward to receiving your cheque in settlement in due course. **(full stop)** As you can see, the outstanding amount is **(pound sign)** two hundred and forty-four pounds and forty pence.

Yours faithfully,

(PAUSE)

Check your work from Model Task fourteen two in your book. I began dictating at . . . .
The next task is a production task for your teacher to mark and you should type it once only. This is a memo incorporating the table given on page 19 of your book. This is Production Task M. Don't forget to time yourself. Ready?

(POINT ON INDEX IS . . .)

MEMO
To   General Manager
From Sales Manager
(heading) MONTHLY SALES FIGURES
I set out below details of the returns by representatives for last month. **(full stop)** The fourth column shows the net increase or decrease compared with the figure for the same month / last ½ year. **(full stop, underscore the words "last year". Typist, now display the table headed "Sales Figures".) (paragraph)**

Some of the above figures need clarification. **(full stop)** Firstly it is clear that the main demand for our products is in the south eastern area of England, which, when one includes London, accounts for approximately half of our total sales. // **1** **(paragraph)**

The figure for the **(initial capitals)** Midlands Area is unusually low. **(full stop)** This, to a large extent, is due to the poor health of the sales representative, Mr. Couch, who was off sick for the last two weeks of the month. **(full stop)** The downward / ½ trend in the Midlands is in fact not as sharp as this figure would suggest. **(paragraph)**

The plus figure for Scotland is really quite remarkable as all our competitors are finding the market there very difficult indeed. **(full stop)** I am sure we // owe our continued good results in **2** that area almost entirely to Mr. McVeigh's tireless efforts. **(full stop)** Mr. McVeigh has won the sales representatives' bonus scheme for seven months out of the last twelve. **(full stop)** I am sure you will agree that this / is a remarkable record, and **½** one which you may wish to mention in your report to the **(initial capitals)** Board of Directors. **(paragraph)**

I should be pleased to discuss the figures with you, if you think this is necessary.

(PAUSE)

Carefully check your work before handing it in for marking. Make sure your name and "Production Task M" are on the top, and make a note of how long you took altogether. Hand in your work for marking.

I shall now dictate short notes from which you are to compose a letter. Before you attempt this task, you should carefully study Reference Section 1 2 in your book. When you are ready to start composing your letter, look at the notes to Task fourteen three in your book. I shall now dictate the short notes for your reply. Are you ready?

(POINT ON INDEX IS ...)

Confirm arrangements OK. Pleased to come for Open Day. Suggest title "Political Consequences of Britain's Entry". Can come any Friday p.m. Always free then for Constituency work. Let me know definite date.

(PAUSE)

When you have finished your own attempt you should compare it with the one set out as the suggested Model Task 1 4.3 in your book, remembering that it cannot possibly be identical.

I shall now dictate short notes from which you are to compose a reply to Household Products Limited. Look at the notes to Task fourteen four for further information. Do not look at the worked example before you start to type or you will be wasting your time and defeating the point of the task. You must compose your own version first. Ready?

(POINT ON INDEX IS ...)

Acknowledge letter and enclosure. Agree it was our mistake. Apologize for previous complaint. Will investigate and make sure no recurrence. Couldn't they put this instruction on the front of the form? Difficult to see small print on the back. Enclose / order for replacements, plus cheque. Ask for latest **½** catalogue and price lists.

(PAUSE)

When you have finished your own attempt, you should compare it with the one in your book.

I shall now dictate short notes from which you are to compose a letter in reply to Mr. Robert Grant. This is Production Task N for your teacher to mark. Make sure that your name is at the top of the paper, and make a note of the time at which you start this task. Ready?

(POINT ON INDEX IS ...)

Acknowledge letter. Sorry to hear about trouble with new machine. Very short-staffed at the moment. However, no excuse for broken appointments. Have asked Service Manager to investigate and improve. Thanks for troubling to write. Trust no further problems.

(PAUSE)

Carefully check your work before handing it in for marking. Make sure your name and "Production Task N" are on the top, and make a note of how long you took altogether. Hand in your work for marking.

End of Unit Fourteen

Unit Fifteen

RSA AUDIO-TYPEWRITING, STAGE II, JUNE 1983

Before each passage you will be told its length and the title or addressee. Further instructions may also be dictated before the passage begins, but before you start typing make sure that you have read the instructions on the printed paper handed to you by the Invigilator. Addresses and references not given in the dictation are printed on that paper.

The first passage is in the nature of a "warming up" test. Although comparatively few marks are allocated to it, you are advised to type it as accurately as possible.

Passage 1 — An article of 150 words

Minutes

Public relations in its many forms is vital to all institutions whether they be trade associations, professional bodies, or research organisations. **(paragraph)**

There is a need to tell the public at large, as well as your own members about your work. **(full stop)** / Possible new members ½ and consumers at home and abroad, as well as employees and other interested persons, need to be kept informed, and each may need a different style of approach. **(full stop)** Your internal news sheet will not be suitable for // the general public, and **1** neither will your annual report. **(paragraph)**

A successful public relations programme does not just happen. **(full stop)** It has to be planned and followed up professionally, just as the budget planning and control programme would be. **(full stop)** When institutes want / reliable financial advice they ½ go to the expert, namely their accountant. **(full stop)** Does this happen to anything like the same extent when it comes to their very important public relations strategy? **(question mark)**

Passage 2 — A letter of 69 words to London Books

Minutes

Dear Sirs

Thank you for your enquiry of ten June requesting details of our publications available to the general public. **(paragraph)**

I enclose a leaflet giving details of all our current publications, together with prices. **(full stop)** You will note that booksellers are / allowed a trade discount of **(figures)** fifteen per cent. ½ **(paragraph)**

We shall be pleased to supply you with any of these publications on receipt of a completed order form.

Yours faithfully

Passage 3 — A letter of 140 words to Miss Janet Cooper

Minutes

Dear Miss Cooper

Thank you for your letter of nine June which followed a note in the February issue of **(open quotes, initial capitals)** "Modern Materials" **(close quotes)** about our periodical **(open quotes, initial capitals)** "Abstracts of International Materials Literature". **(close quotes, full stop)** I have pleasure in enclosing details of the volume produced / during nineteen ½ eighty-two, and also that being produced during the current year. **(paragraph)**

(Open quotes, initial capital) "Abstracts" **(close quotes)** is produced as a result of searching technical publications from world- **(hyphen)** wide sources and the scope of "Abstracts" is being progressively widened to include an increasing // number **1** of items on plastics. **(paragraph)**

I also enclose leaflets about our other publications, including technical information broadsheets, conference report books, and translations. **(full stop)** These latter are available only to member companies, but we should be delighted to enrol your organization as / an associate member if you so wish, and I| ½ enclose details of our associate membership arrangements.

Yours sincerely
Publications Manager

Passage 4 — A letter of 154 words to Mr V Godjal

Minutes

Dear Sir

Thank you for your letter of two June. **(full stop)** We are pleased to note your interest in our booklet on **(initial capitals)** Engineering Data on Materials. **(full stop)** This is available in both|**(capitals)**|SI and|**(initial capitals)**|Imperial Units but can only be supplied / on a sale basis. **(full stop)** A leaflet is enclosed ½ giving details. **(paragraph)**

We regret that we can only supply publications to addresses overseas on receipt of the appropriate remittance, and we are therefore also enclosing our pro forma **(P R O space F O R M A)** invoice to cover the // supply of one each of the booklets. **(full 1 stop)** The prices given in the leaflet cover postage and packing by surface mail, but, as we have had repeated problems with items sent by surface mail failing to arrive at their destination in / India, we have taken the liberty of adding an air mail charge ½ as we find this a more reliable service. **(paragraph)**

If we can be of any further assistance, please let us know.

Yours faithfully

Passage 5 – A letter of 122 words to Mr James Findlay

Minutes

Dear Sir
Thank you for your letter concerning translations of papers appearing in the foreign language technical press. **(paragraph)**

We only commission translations of papers which we think will be of general interest to our members, and a list of those / currently available is enclosed. **(full stop)** If any member company requests a translation of a particular paper not on the list we have to ask the member concerned to bear the full commercial costs of the translation, unless it is one which // we have already earmarked for translation. **(paragraph)** **1**

If you would advise us which particular papers you are interested in, we can let you know whether we intend to commission a translation. **(full stop)** Otherwise we will give you a quotation for obtaining one. / **½**

Yours faithfully

Passage 6 – A memorandum of 191 words to Dr P R Henderson

Minutes

I have repeatedly drawn the attention of secretaries of subcommittees to the requirement that reports for discussion at subcommittees must be circulated before the meeting, preferably giving the members two weeks in which to read them before attending the meeting. **(full stop)** / I appreciate that **½**
problems sometimes arise and have given instructions that, if a report cannot be circulated two weeks before the subcommittee meeting, I should be informed as early as possible that there is likely to be a problem. **(full stop)** I // can then make **1**
sure that everyone is alerted and that the best efforts are made by all concerned to retrieve the situation. **(paragraph)**

I was very surprised, therefore, on attending a recent meeting of the **(initial capitals)** Quality Control Subcommittee, to find that / three out of the four reports to be discussed were all **½**
tabled. **(full stop)** I had not been informed of any difficulty nor that these papers would not be circulated in advance. **(paragraph)**

I regard the failure to circulate the documents as a // serious **2**
discourtesy to members of the subcommittee, and I would like to have some comment as to why I was not informed and an assurance that this will not happen again.

Passage 7 – A letter of 124 words to Mrs H Small

Minutes

Dear Madam
Thank you for your letter of eight June drawing our attention to the discrepancy in colour between the quilt cover and the curtains we sent you. **(paragraph)**

We have checked our stocks of the curtains and confirm that those / labelled pink are indeed brown. **(full stop)** We have **½**
now taken this up with our suppliers and expect to receive new stocks of pink curtains in the near future. **(paragraph)**

In the meantime perhaps you would be good enough to return the brown // curtains by parcel post, using the **(capitals)** **1**
FREEPOST address label enclosed, and we will forward replacement pink curtains when we receive these. **(paragraph)**

We apologize for the inconvenience caused and hope that you will be completely happy with the matching curtains when / **½**
they arrive.

Yours faithfully

Passage 8 – Notes for reply to the letter on page 4 of your printed paper

Minutes

Regret subscription rate quoted correct. General increase in subscription rates due to rising level of claims caused by increased medical costs. Also come into high subscription band now husband over fifty. No reduction possible as maximum fifteen per cent discount already / received. Might consider transferring to new **(initial capitals)** Hospital Care Only scheme which subscribers are finding attractive. Details of all schemes enclosed. **(60 words)** **½**

End of Unit Fifteen

Unit Sixteen

RSA AUDIO-TYPEWRITING, STAGE II, MAY 1984

Before each passage you will be told its length and the title or addressee. Further instructions may also be dictated before the passage begins, but before you start typing make sure that you have read the instructions on the printed paper handed to you by the Invigilator. Addresses and references not given in the dictation are printed on that paper.

The first passage is in the nature of a "warming up" test. Although comparatively few marks are allocated to it, you are advised to type it as accurately as possible.

Passage 1 – An article of 150 words

Minutes

The south- **(hyphen)** east coast of England faces the continent of Europe. **(full stop)** It is the part of England which the French can see from their cliffs and the first view of England seen by many travellers from abroad. **(paragraph)**

Eight thousand years / ago England was joined to the conti- ½ nent. **(full stop)** The sea then broke through and eroded the chalk, which left Britain an island and formed the well-**(hyphen)** known white cliffs of the south-east coast. **(paragraph)**

Brighton today is the largest town on // this coast, but before **1** **(figures)** seventeen hundred and fifty it was a place only for sailors and fishermen, as few other people ever visited it. **(full stop)** After the introduction of the railways in the nineteenth century and the idea that sea bathing / was good for health, ½ excursions to the coast became popular and many English saw the sea for the first time. **(full stop)** By eighteen hundred Brighton had grown into a seaside resort.

Passage 2 – Notes for reply to the letter on page 4 of your printed paper

Minutes

Two places available period requested. Both owners going overseas on educational exchange. One four-bedroomed house with central heating; other accommodation two-bedroomed flat, with storage heaters, in quiet road very near to centre. Enclose particulars. If other suitable property / ½ becomes available will contact. Rented property in area difficult to obtain.

(51 words)

Passage 3 – A memorandum of 95 words to Head of Bio-Engineering

Minutes

When I visited St Peter's Hospital in London recently, I was shown a new micro- **(hyphen)** computer which is able to measure how much blood a patient's heart is pumping each minute. **(full stop)** This machine costs **(pound sign)** four hundred and I would / very much like to purchase one without ½ delay. **(paragraph)**

If this micro-computer proves to be as advantageous as I am convinced it is, I would eventually like to purchase twelve more machines, one for each of the beds in the // **1** intensive-**(hyphen)** care unit. **(paragraph)**

I enclose a leaflet showing this machine together with my requisition form.

Passage 4 – A letter of 230 words to Mr W North

Minutes

Dear Mr. North

Thank you very much for your enquiry regarding franchises and I hope the following information will be of interest to you and useful. **(paragraph)**

Many companies nowadays – **(dash)** over two hundred and fifty in fact – **(dash)** run franchise operations. **(full stop)** Their / goods and services range from hamburgers to printing; ½ **(semi-colon)** drain cleaning to bridal gowns. **(full stop)** Franchising is a way companies can expand and keep their capital costs down. **(paragraph)**

In order to buy a franchise you will need some capital; **(semi-colon)** the amount depends // on which franchise you wish to **1** buy. **(full stop)** If you wish to buy a **(open double quotes)** "bridal gown" **(close double quotes)** franchise you will have to give the main company, for example, **(pound sign)** fifteen thousand. **(full stop)** With this money the company selects a suitable vacant shop, decorates / it in its colours and stocks it ½ with its gowns. **(full stop)** The people chosen, called franchisees, (F R A N C H I S E E S) generally go through a short period of training at the company's **(initial capitals)** Head Office, and for the first few weeks someone from Head Office helps you // to run your shop. **(paragraph)** **2**

The main company takes an agreed percentage of your turnover, usually about ten per cent. **(full stop)** It ought to be remembered that it will take some years to recover the initial outlay and that there is no / guarantee of success. **(paragraph)** ½

Lastly, it is wise not to sign up for a franchise without the approval of your solicitor or accountant.

Yours sincerely
Praxiteles Chamber of Commerce
David Young

Passage 5 – A letter of 145 words to P T Thomas
Minutes

Dear Mr. Thomas

We thank you for replying to our advertisement and enclose a free copy of our **(initial capital)** Guide for your inspection. **(paragraph)**

The Guide was set up about ten years ago because it was felt that low- **(hyphen)** priced shares offered / the best area of ½ profit for the investor in stocks and shares. **(full stop)** If we take a look at the ten outstanding companies in the country today, no fewer than eight companies were mentioned in our Guide over the last three // years. **(paragraph)**   1

We select companies that we feel are under- **(hyphen)** performing but which could with new management and modernization of plant and machinery become successful and prosperous. **(paragraph)**

The Guide is published annually, but we hope in the near future to publish / it more frequently. **(full stop)** If you know any ½ company which could be included in our Guide please let us know.

Yours sincerely
T Baxter
Assistant Editor

Passage 6 – A report of 180 words
Minutes

The **(initial capitals)** International Food Exhibition was held recently at **(initial capital)** Olympia (O L Y M P I A) and it was organized by the **(initial capitals)** British Farm Produce Council. **(full stop)** It was Britain's third Exhibition which tried to equal those held by our European counterparts. **(paragraph)**

The first **(capitals)** IFE, held / in nineteen hundred and eighty- ½ two, was a small success; **(semi-colon)** the second, held the following year, was more successful, but the third Exhibition, held two months ago, broke all records. **(full stop)** Because of the huge support it has received from food //manufacturing 1 companies, it seems to have become an established annual event. **(paragraph)**

Overseas firms, mainly from Denmark and Ireland, said that they liked the compactness of the Exhibition and found the organization much more efficient than the German and French counterparts. / **(paragraph)**   ½

The Exhibition provided opportunities for large and small wholesalers and retailers not only to see fresh and processed products in one small area but to see them displayed in attractive surroundings showing what could be done in a shop. **(paragraph)**

The // problem now facing the organizers is whether the present 2 site can cope with the expansion programme which will undoubtedly follow.

Passage 7 – A circular letter of 95 words
Minutes

I am pleased to welcome you to **(initial capitals)** Praxiteles College here in London and am enclosing a booklet giving a comprehensive cover of various aspects of College life, which I hope you will read thoroughly. **(paragraph)**

In addition to meeting / your educational and training require- ½ ments, the College has a large number of overseas students. **(full stop)** I hope you will take this opportunity to meet them and gain a considerable knowledge and understanding of their countries and customs. **(paragraph)**

Finally I would like // to wish you success and happiness whilst 1 you are at this College.

Yours sincerely
Principal

Passage 8 – A letter of 55 words to the Manager
Minutes

Dear Sir

We enclose a copy of our **(initial capitals)** Accounts for the last financial year which ended on twenty-fourth February nineteen hundred and eighty-four. **(paragraph)**

Would you kindly note that we have decided not to go ahead with the purchase / of a computer, which we discussed with ½ you some time ago.

Yours faithfully
James Brown

End of Unit Sixteen

Model Answers to Production Tasks

Production Task A

I hope you are enjoying your first lesson.

There will be many good jobs open to you.

You will find advertisements in all the newspapers.

You can earn a very good salary.

I think you will find the work interesting.

Production Task B

We apologise for the delay in replying to your letter which we received only today.

The goods you require are not in stock and will not be delivered until next month.

In the meantime we could send you some similar styles which are certain to meet with your approval.

If you would like us to forward these items please telephone our local branch immediately.

We are sorry we cannot meet your exact requirements but hope our suggestion will help you.

Production Task C

At the recent Annual General Meeting of British Products Limited the Chairman presented the Report and Accounts for the year.

The Chairman said that the figures for the year were very good indeed. He pointed out that the Company had done considerably better than other firms manufacturing similar products. This was a very satisfactory result after the disappointing figures for last year.

The Chairman continued by saying that he thought there was considerable potential for further growth of the Company. He thanked the Directors and all the employees of the Company for their hard work. He concluded by saying that progress was only possible when there was loyalty and enthusiasm among staff at all levels.

Production Task D

There have been a number of bankruptcies in our town in the last few years and many people have become unemployed. So far our own company has survived several major crises.

Many companies have closed down and this affects the trade for local shops and services. Firms may get into financial difficulties. Fortunately our business is not affected by a general slump in trade.

We hope that business prospects generally will improve soon. There will be a need for much investment in declining cities and other localities. There will need to be an improvement in the facilities we offer to other businesses.

Production Task E

Computers are becoming cheaper. In fact a small home computer is very powerful when compared with its predecessors only ten years ago. Personal computers can now do the tasks which previously would have needed computers big enough to fill an entire room, costing thousands of pounds, and requiring several highly trained operators.

We are only at the beginning of the computer revolution. We can expect more and more areas of our lives to be affected by computer use. Usually the changes arrive without much fuss(,) and often without us even realising that major changes in technology have happened. In the past two decades(,) we have grown used to pocket calculators, cashpoint machines at the banks, information systems linked to our televisions, and visual display units everywhere.

An expert on computer development, Mrs Jane Windsor, has predicted that computers will eventually affect all aspects of our lives by the end of the century. Mr Brian Green, a computer consultant to many major companies, believes that the UK will continue to play a leading world role in the development of software.

Production Task F

KAB/--

Date

Turner & Black Ltd
34-38 Belding Road
Huddersfield
HD2 3MA

Dear Sirs

AGENCY SERVICES

We have pleasure in announcing details of our new
Copying Service. We have a full range of equipment
for printing, offset duplicating and photocopying.
Our charges are very reasonable as you will see from
the enclosed price list.

May we remind you that we continue to offer our
services as an Employment Agency for both your
permanent and temporary staff requirements. With
the present shortage of trained staff, you may have
difficulties in recruiting suitable people. If so,
we invite you to contact the Manager, Mrs Short, who
will be pleased to help you.

Yours faithfully
OFFICE PERSONNEL LIMITED

K A Bond
Director

Enc

Production Task G

PERS/ID/--

Date

Miss P Jeffries
46 Laburnum Rd
Croydon
Surrey
CR4 2BB

Dear Miss Jeffries

Thank you for attending the interview here yesterday. I am very pleased to
confirm that I can offer you the position of secretary to the Deputy
Manager. The hours of work are 0930 to 1700 hrs Monday to Friday: one hour
is allowed for lunch.

I confirm that your annual salary will be eight thousand pounds plus
luncheon vouchers of seventy-five pence per day. You will be allowed to
take annual holidays of four weeks altogether (but not more than two weeks
may be taken consecutively).

Would you please report direct to Mr Rostron at 1000 hrs next Monday
morning. Please bring with you your tax documents.

I enclose a cheque for £2.10 for your travelling expenses in connection
with the interview. I look forward to working with you and hope that you
will let me know immediately if at any time you have problems connected
with your employment.

Yours sincerely

Personnel Manager

Enc

(Note - also accept 4 weeks and 2 weeks)

Production Task H

```
MEMO

To     Company Secretary              Ref    MN/POJ

From   Sales Manager                  Date
```

GENERAL ENGINEERING LIMITED: ANNUAL DINNER

I confirm our telephone conversation of this morning and am attaching 2 complimentary tickets for the Annual Exhibition and Dinner of General Engineering Limited at the Grand Hotel, Kings Road. As mentioned, I have an important last-minute engagement and cannot attend personally.

It should be a very pleasant evening, but I suggest you look through the appropriate files before you go in case anything concerning business crops up. My main contact with General Engineering is Mr Robert Jenkinson, the Sales Director. My secretary telephoned him explaining that you will be coming in my place. Mr Jenkinson said that he would meet you at 8 pm in the Reception Area of the Hotel.

Enc

(NOTE - also accept King´s Road and Secretary.)

Production Task I

Our ref   Sales/RJT
Your ref GB/OT

Date

Miss G Bolch
15 Long Street
London
SW8 4ES

Dear Miss Bolch

Thank you for your letter of yesterday's date, enclosing your order. Unfortunately, we no longer manufacture the range of women's swimsuits you require. The models you have chosen are from last year's catalogue.

We are enclosing our new catalogue which shows our Company's latest designs. We are sure you will agree that we have an excellent range and that you will find some suitable styles. You can order direct from us, enclosing your firm's cheque for the appropriate amount, or you can ask our Representative to call on you. Our Representative's name is Mr Robert James, and the Company's telephone number is given above. He will be very pleased to hear from you.

Yours sincerely

SALES MANAGER

Enc

Production Task J

SHORTAGE OF SECRETARIAL STAFF

Britain´s export trade is being affected by a shortage of trained secretaries. The Assistant Director of the Export Council for Britain said that most companies were experiencing difficulty in obtaining good, bi-lingual secretaries. In the past, it was not difficult to hire suitable staff to meet their needs. The principal reason for the shortage is that far more opportunities exist for intelligent women nowadays: there are a larger number of careers from which to choose.

To ensure a larger supply of good secretaries, salaries will have to be a good deal higher than formerly. Career opportunities within the business world will also have to be widened. This will enable the more capable women to set their sights on managerial jobs. If nothing is done to raise the promotion prospects of women entering their employment, commercial organizations will lose the best workers to other professions.

Production Task K

DRAFT

Month, Year

Dear Madam

SUMMER SALES CAMPAIGN

Thank you for your recent application to join our team of sales
demonstration staff for our 3rd national sales campaign. We should
like you to attend for interview at the following address and time:

If you are recruited to the team you will be required to wear our
smart, fashionable suit at all times when on Company business. You
will be provided with a white Ford Escort car and, in this connection,
should bring your driving licence to the interview. You must be
prepared to travel extensively throughout the campaign and to work
overtime if required. Would you please confirm whether you will
attend the interview at the time stated above.

Yours faithfully
PRESIDENT CIGARETTE COMPANY LIMITED

John Austin
SALES MANAGER

Passage 1 RSA I, May 1984

SR/KG

8 May 1984

Miss S Lawson
49 Princes Ave
Hull
HU6 7DR

Dear Miss Lawson

With reference to your interview at this office yesterday, I confirm that I am prepared to offer you the position of Junior Clerical Assistant as from Monday, 21 May. You will be working for my Private Secretary, Miss Karen Green, whom you met yesterday.

As was pointed out at the interview, the starting salary (paid on a monthly basis) is £4,000, and annual increments are £500. Luncheon vouchers are also given to all staff each week.

I am enclosing a booklet setting out the terms and conditions of service, and may I suggest that you read this carefully and keep it by you for future reference.

As was mentioned at the interview, I confirm that I will make arrangements for you to attend the local College of Further Education on a day-release basis, to further your secretarial and business studies qualifications. When you come to the office on the Monday morning, ask at the reception desk for Miss Green and she will come to meet you.

We look forward to your joining the Company and hope that you will be happy with us.

Yours sincerely

S Robinson
PERSONNEL OFFICER

Enc

Passage 2

MEMORANDUM

From	Personnel Manager	Ref	
To	Ms Karen Green	Date	8 May 1984

As you know, we appointed Sandra Lawson yesterday as your new assistant — she is starting on Monday, 21 May, and I said you would meet her at Reception when she arrives.

Please plan an induction programme for Sandra, covering the first month of her employment with the Company, and also write to the local College of Further Education asking for particulars of day-release courses in secretarial and business studies. She already has some basic knowledge of micro-computers and word processors and has expressed a desire to study this field in more detail. Please mention this in your letter to the College, as they run specialist courses in these subjects.

Passage 3

LANDSCAPING AND DISPLAY OF PLANTS IN OFFICES

Many office buildings now have an open-plan layout in place of many smaller rooms enclosed by walls. It is usual practice to divide such a large office into several smaller working areas, and plants are an attractive way of doing this. Plants make such a difference to the appearance of rooms that contain only desks, chairs and filing cabinets - they help to create a pleasant working environment and brighten up the room. Plants are especially effective in reception areas where they give a welcome and convey a sense of care and interest.

Care should be taken to position the plants so that they do not interfere with the movements of office personnel. Therefore plants grouped together in varying heights make a more effective display than those placed individually. Furthermore they grow better when grouped together, as the humidity around them is increased.

Water used in either a small pool or a fountain may make an attractive feature when landscaping, and also provides the surrounding plants with moist air to grow, and this is better for them.

Passage 4

8 May 1984

Mr D Edwards
Computer Management Plc
244 Heads Road
GRIMSBY
South Humberside
DO30 16DP

Dear Mr Edwards

I confirm my telephone conversation with you this morning and set out below the arrangements we made regarding the landscaping of your open-plan offices.

1   My staff will commence work at 8 am on Friday next.

2   The work will take approximately six hours to complete.

3   A florist will call each Friday morning to maintain the plants and shrubs.

Good luck with your new micro-computing venture.

Yours sincerely

PRAXITELES LANDSCAPE GARDENERS

<u>Supreme Sale of Plants and Bulbs</u>

C o m e   E a r l y

Saturday, 19 May 1984, 10 am – 2 pm

in the Main Hall, Central Avenue, Scarborough

HARDY AZALEAS (Various)	£1.25 each plant
CLEMATIS PLANTS (Nelly Moser, Ville de Lyon, Jackmanii)	£1.25 each plant
HARDY GARDEN CAMELLIAS (varied stock)	£1.00 each plant
HONEYSUCKLE (scented varieties)	£1.50 each plant
MAGNOLIA TREES	£6.00 each tree
DOUBLE BEGONIAS (mixed)	5 for £1.00
DECORATIVE AND BORDER DAHLIAS (mixed colours)	6 for £1.20
GLADIOLI CORMS (packs of 100) (28" high")	£1.00
MIXED SHRUBS (many from varieties in stock)	from £1.00 each shrub

ALSO A LARGE COLLECTION OF ANNUALS

FOR SUMMER FLOWERING THIS SEASON

LARGE CAR PARKS NEARBY

Production Task L

MEMO

To   Sales Manager
        Accounts Manager
        London Area Manager

From   Managing Director   Date

SALES MEETINGS

It was decided at a recent meeting of the Board that the Sales Department Manager should hold official meetings with the Accounts Department Manager on a regular basis, so that there is better liaison on matters relating to customers´ accounts, credit limits, etc. Area Sales Managers may also be invited to attend if items affecting their specific areas are to be discussed.

Accordingly, would you please arrange to attend the first of these meetings to be held in the Board Room next Wednesday at 1430 hrs. The agenda will be as follows:

A G E N D A

1   Reports and matters arising

2   Analysis of new accounts

3   Discount rates for the London Area

4   Credit limits in view of recent restrictions

5   Any other business

Would you please prepare the appropriate reports for the first item on the agenda. These meetings will be held on the first Wednesday of each month, so please arrange your appointments accordingly.

Production Task M

MEMO

```
To     General Manager
From   Sales Manager                    Date
```

MONTHLY SALES FIGURES

I set out below details of the returns by representatives for last month.
The fourth column shows the net increase or decrease compared with the figure
for the same month last year.

Area	Representative	Sales £	Increase/ Decrease
London	Mr A Jepson	5735	+421
Midlands	Mr R Couch	3891	−403
N Ireland	Mr F Shackleton	1871	−118
North	Miss S Longbotham	2872	− 46
Scotland	Mr A McVeigh	1976	+ 39
South East	Mrs D Collinson	5942	+634
South West	Mr P Quiller	3641	+ 48
Wales	Mr S Robertson	1872	− 34

Some of the figures need clarification. Firstly it is clear that the main
demand for our products is in the south eastern area of England which, when
one includes London, accounts for approximately half our total sales.

The figure for the Midlands Area is unusually low. This to a large extent is
due to the poor health of the sales representative, Mr Couch, who was off
sick for the last 2 weeks of the month. The downward trend in the Midlands
is in fact not as sharp as this figure would suggest.

The plus figure for Scotland is really quite remarkable as all our
competitors are finding the market there very difficult indeed. I am sure we
owe our continued good results in that area almost entirely to Mr McVeigh's
tireless efforts. Mr McVeigh has won the sales representatives' bonus scheme
for 7 months out of the last 12. I am sure you will agree that this is a
remarkable record, and one which you may wish to mention in your report to
the Board of Directors.

I should be pleased to discuss the figures with you, if you think this is
necessary.

Production Task N

This task is a letter from notes, composed by the student, in reply to
Task 7:2. The notes dicatated are:

Acknowledge letter. Sorry to hear about trouble with new machine.
Very short-staffed at the moment. However no excuse for broken
appointments. Have asked Service Manager to investigate and improve.
Thanks for troubling to write. Trust no further problems.

Passage 1 RSA II, May 1984

The south-east coast of England faces the continent of Europe. It is the
part of England which the French can see from their cliffs and the first
view of England seen by many travellers from abroad.

Eight thousand years ago England was joined to the continent. The sea then
broke through and eroded the chalk, which left Britain an island and formed
the well-known white cliffs of the south-east coast.

Brighton today is the largest town on this coast, but before 1750 it was a
place only for sailors and fishermen, as few other people ever visited it.
After the introduction of the railways in the 19th century and the idea
that sea bathing was good for health, excursions to the coast became
popular and many English saw the sea for the first time. By 1800 Brighton
had grown into a seaside resort.

Passage 2

NORFOLK ESTATE AGENTS

20 College Road

NORWICH

Date

Mrs E Parsons
9145 South Damen
Chicago
Illinois
IL 80202
United States of America

Dear Madam

Thank you for your letter of 24 April 1984 requesting information on
properties for rent in this area.

There are two places available for the period you mention. In both cases
the owners are going overseas on educational exchange. The first is a
four-bedroomed house with central heating. The second is a two-bedroomed
flat, with storage heaters, situated in a quiet road very near to the
centre. I enclose particulars of both properties.

I am sorry to say that it is generally difficult to obtain rented property
in this area. If other suitable property becomes available, I will of
course contact you.

Yours faithfully
NORWICH ESTATE AGENTS

MANAGER

Encs

Passage 3

MEMORANDUM

From	Mr M Turner	Ref	
To	Head of Bio-Engineering	Date	15 May 1984

When I visited St Peter's Hospital in London recently, I was shown a new micro-computer which is able to measure how much blood a patient's heart is pumping each minute. This machine costs £400 and I would very much like to purchase one without delay.

If this micro-computer proves to be as advantageous as I am convinced it is, I would eventually like to purchase twelve more machines, one for each of the beds in the intensive-care unit.

I enclose a leaflet showing this machine together with my requisition form.

Encs

Passage 4

DY/NC

Date

Mr W North
5 Church Lane
EXETER
ER2 3EA

Dear Mr North

FRANCHISES

Thank you very much for your enquiry regarding franchises and I hope the following information will be of interest to you and useful.

Many companies nowadays — over two hundred and fifty in fact — run franchise operations. Their goods and services range from hamburgers to printing; drain cleaning to bridal gowns. Franchising is a way companies can expand and keep their capital costs down.

In order to buy a franchise you will need some capital; the amount depends on which franchise you wish to buy. If you wish to buy a "bridal gown" franchise you will have to give the main company, for example, £15,000. With this money the company selects a suitable vacant shop, decorates it in its own colours and stocks it with its gowns. The people chosen, called franchisees, generally go through a short period of training at the company's Head Office, and for the first few weeks someone from Head Office helps you to run your shop.

The main company takes an agreed percentage of your turnover, usually about ten per cent. It ought to be remembered that it will take some years to recover the initial outlay and that there is no guarantee of success.

Lastly, it is wise not to sign up for a franchise without the approval of your solicitor or accountant.

Yours sincerely
PRAXITELES CHAMBER OF COMMERCE

David Young

Passage 5

TB/MF

Date

Mr P T Thomas
6 Sandalwood Avenue
BROMLEY
Kent
BY3 7RH

Dear Mr Thomas

PRAXITELES SHARE GUIDE

We thank you for replying to our advertisement and enclose a free copy of
our Guide for your inspecton.

The Guide was set up about ten years ago because it was felt that
low-priced shares offered the best area of profit for the investor in
stocks and shares. If we take a look at the 10 outstanding companies in
the country today, no fewer than 8 companies were mentioned in our Guide
over the last 3 years.

We select companies that we feel are under-performing but which could with
new management and modernisation of plant and machinery become successful
and prosperous.

The Guide is published annually, but we hope in the near future to publish
it more frequently. If you know any company which could be included in our
Guide please let us know.

Yours sincerely

T Baxter
ASSISTANT EDITOR

Enc

Passage 6

INTERNATIONAL FOOD EXHIBITION

The International Food Exhibition was held recently at Olympia and it was organized by the British Farm Produce Council. It was Britain´s third Exhibition which tried to equal those held by our European counterparts. The first IFE, held in 1982, was a small success; the second, held the following year, was more successful, but the third Exhibition, held two months ago, broke all records. Because of the huge support it has received from food manufacturing companies, it seems to have become an established annual event.

Overseas firms, mainly from Denmark and Ireland, said that they liked the compactness of the Exhibition and found the organization much more efficient than the German and French counterparts.

The Exhibition provided opportunities for large and small wholesalers and retailers not only to see fresh and processed products in one small area, but to see them displayed in attractive surroundings showing what could be done in a shop.

The problem now facing the organizers is whether the present site can cope with the expansion programme which will undoubtedly follow.

Passage 7

Date as Postmark

Dear Student

I am pleased to welcome you to Praxiteles College here in London and am
enclosing a booklet giving a comprehensive cover of various aspects of
College life, which I hope you will read thoroughly.

In addition to meeting your educational and training requirements, the
College has a large number of overseas students. I hope you will take this
opportunity to meet them and gain a considerable knowledge and
understanding of their countries and customs.

Finally I would like to wish you success and happiness whilst you are at
this College.

Yours sincerely

Principal

Enc

Passage 8

JB/wa

Date

The Manager
Praxi Bank plc
120 Main Road
Mablethorpe
Lincs

Dear Sir

We enclose a copy of our Accounts for the last financial year
which ended on 24 February 1984.

Would you kindly note that we have decided not to go ahead
with the purchase of a computer, which we discussed with you
some time ago.

Yours faithfully

James Brown

Enc

Passage 9

TRADING AND PROFIT AND LOSS ACCOUNT
FOR THE YEAR ENDED 24 FEBRUARY 1984

	£	£
Sales		306,150
Purchases	264,090	
End stock – increase	–	
– decrease	2,870	
Cost of Sales		266,960
Gross Profit		39,190
Bank charges	730	
Cleaning	910	
Hire Purchase interest	510	
Insurances and licences	400	
Lighting and heating	1,470	
Motor expenses	1,340	
Postage, stationery and advertising	500	
Professional charges – accountancy	350	
– stocktaking	210	
Rates and water rates	2,980	
Repairs and renewals – property	–	
– general	1,600	
Sundry trade expenses	310	
Telephone	310	
Wages and National Insurance	20,660	
Wrapping paper	370	
Overhead expenses		32,650
		6,540
Depreciation:–		
Furniture and Fittings	740	
Refrigerator	200	
Bacon slicer	170	
Motor vehicles	2,880	
		3,990
Net Profit for the year		£2,550